T0334264

How to Structure a Thesis, Report or Paper

How to Structure a Thesis, Report or Paper provides concise, practical guidance for students to help make their writing more structured at any level. It assists students in demonstrating what they have learned in the relevant course or degree programme in a way that is accessible to the supervisor and the examiner.

Drawing on almost 20 years of supervision experience, the author presents the eight sections of a well-structured thesis, report or paper, together with discussing other relevant issues. Each chapter provides a detailed description of why each section of a thesis, report or paper is structured in the way it is, and its relationship to the whole piece of work. Good and bad examples are provided throughout the book, and there is a focus on key areas such as the six parts of an Introduction and its relationship to the Conclusion, how to phrase clear research questions and hypotheses to the use of references and how to make the thesis, report or paper easier to read. The structure presented in this book can be used to support many courses on the student's entire degree programme, as the structure can be adapted by re-arranging or deleting sections.

This book is an invaluable aid to students at all stages in higher education, from their first report or paper until they write their final thesis. It provides clear guidelines for when students should ask their supervisors for advice, and when students can use their own initiatives to learn the most. It makes writing a thesis, report or paper more straightforward!

Robert P. Ormrod, Ph.D., is Associate Professor, Department of Management, School of Business and Social Sciences, Aarhus University, Denmark. He has supervised hundreds of students over the past 20 years. During this time, he developed a guide to structuring theses, reports and papers. His students found it so useful that they encouraged him to write a book about it.

How to Structure a Thesis, Report or Paper

A Guide for Students

Robert P. Ormrod

Routledge
Taylor & Francis Group

LONDON AND NEW YORK

Cover image: 3pod / Getty Images

First published 2023
by Routledge
4 Park Square, Milton Park, Abingdon, Oxon OX14 4RN

and by Routledge
605 Third Avenue, New York, NY 10158

Routledge is an imprint of the Taylor & Francis Group, an informa business

© 2023 Robert P. Ormrod

British Library Cataloguing-in-Publication Data
A catalogue record for this book is available from the British Library

Library of Congress Cataloging-in-Publication Data
A catalog record for this book has been requested

ISBN: 978-1-032-36948-8 (hbk)
ISBN: 978-1-032-36946-4 (pbk)
ISBN: 978-1-003-33463-7 (ebk)

DOI: 10.4324/9781003334637

Typeset in Galliard
by Apex CoVantage, LLC

Dedicated to my students – past, present and future

Contents

How to structure a thesis, report or paper

I have taught at universities for almost 20 years, and in that time I have had the pleasure of supervising several hundred under- and postgraduate students whilst they have written their bachelor's and master's theses, internship reports or semester papers. One thing that has always struck me is how very few of them had been taught how to structure a thesis, report or paper. I was never taught myself, but as soon as I realised how a simple structure could help, writing a thesis, report or paper became much more straightforward. Not easier, just more straightforward.

I started to think about how I could help my students develop a structure for their work – not just when I was supervising them but also afterwards in their careers after their time in higher education. Initially, I discussed the elements of a thesis, report and paper with my students. As time went on and I became more experienced, I created a document that my students and I went through at our first meeting. After I taught a seminar to undergraduate students with the aim of helping them with the structure of their first piece of writing at my university, pretty much all of them said that they had learned something that would help them throughout their time in higher education, and probably beyond. When I told some of them that I was considering

DOI: 10.4324/9781003334637-1

writing a book on the subject, the response was clear: the sooner, the better. And here is that book.

So why is it a good idea to have a structure for your work before you start writing it, even before you develop the first draft of a research question? First of all, it makes your life more straightforward – not necessarily easier but more straightforward. By dividing your work into smaller, more manageable sections, it is possible to focus on a specific topic, such as your method or the results of your investigation. On balance, it is easier to write a short section of a thesis, report or paper than concentrating on the whole piece of work in one go, as you have less to remember.

Imagine the writing process as driving on a motorway. You start writing when you drive onto the motorway, and the finished product is when you drive off the motorway at your destination. Along the motorway, there are times when the motorway splits to head towards different destinations, and here it is useful to have a map – a clear structure – to help you work out which lane of the motorway you are supposed to be in to get to your destination of choice. It's not only you who gets the benefit of a clear structure – your supervisor and the person grading your work will also benefit from an easy-to-follow and logical structure.

Supervisors

Good supervisors recognise that each student is different. If there are 20 students in your class or on your degree programme, your supervisor has to balance 20 different pieces of work written by 20 very different people, each with a different background, different strengths and weaknesses, different ambitions and different future career plans.

I regularly supervise 30 students during a semester who write everything from short internship reports to master's theses, so you can see it takes a lot of time and energy to keep on top of what all of my students are doing. It helps if they state the topic of their work at the beginning of each email they send to me, as this makes my life so much easier. This is the first piece of advice in this book – you have just learned something that you can do that will make your supervisor happier! This is a good thing.

My own style of supervision

Supervision sessions vary according to the requirements of your institution and supervisor preferences. Some supervisors prefer to hold group discussions, where students comment on each other's work and gain inspiration from the interaction. I usually supervise individual papers, primarily because of the confidentiality issues associated with the information provided by the commercial organisations that my students often work with. The following details how I supervise my students; your supervisor may be very different, but this is a result of their experience as to what works well for them. Remember, there are two people who have to be comfortable for a successful supervision to occur, both you and your supervisor. In the following I'll give you an idea about how I prefer to organise (or structure, if you will) the supervision process.

I usually start with two in-person meetings that occur a week apart. In the first meeting, I discuss the structure of the paper with my student, what needs to be covered in the Introduction (Chapter 2 in this book), any ideas my student has about which literature is relevant (Chapter 3 in this book), the appropriate methodology and method (Chapter 4 in this book) and their thoughts on alternative research questions. I also take this opportunity to make sure that my student is relaxed about working with me, so that their focus is on what they themselves think and they don't try to second-guess what I want to hear.

At the end of the first meeting, I ask my student to do three things ahead of the second meeting: 1) write a first draft of the Introduction; 2) write their thoughts about the relevant literature, methodology and method down in bullet points; and 3) propose three or four alternative research questions. The second meeting then consists of discussing the Introduction, merging the suggested research questions into one research question, and looking for literature in my institution's online article database. This is all carried out on the student's computer, so there is less to be remembered and more to be learned. Basically, the second meeting focuses on 'fleshing out' the structure and making it clear to my student exactly what they should do, so they can have a running start on writing their thesis, report or paper.

The remainder of the meetings are divided up into those meetings that I consider to be compulsory, and those meetings that the student asks for. Whereas I prefer to hold both of the first two meetings in person, subsequent meetings can be held online, and sometimes even a quick question by e-mail is enough to help my student move on with their work. After the two introductory meetings, I like to meet with my student when they are in the process of writing their Literature Overview section, just before they start on their investigation, and when they are ready to start working with the outcome of their investigation.

My student can also ask for a meeting whenever they feel the need for supervision, although I will say no and explain why if I think that they are asking for too much help. The reason for this is that I cannot remember every thesis, report and paper that I am supervising (and this goes for your own supervisor too). My student knows where they are in the process, but I can only give a response to the specific question that my student asks. In other words, I don't have all of the information, so my answer may be right for the question but wrong for the entire thesis, report or paper. Of course, if my student really needs help then they will get it, but it's always better to try yourself first!

I also almost never read and comment on large sections of text that my students have written. Instead of preventing my student from being independent, I ask my student to write down their questions and uncertainties, and we have a supervision meeting where the student asks me these questions. Of course, me being me, I never give them any answers! I simply ask them what they think the answer is. Whilst this may seem strange, there is a good reason for this.

Think about it this way: you are the one who has done all of the work, and when you explain your problem to your supervisor, you have to say the problem aloud. At this point, I usually ask my student what they think the answer is. My student then tells me what they think. Again, by vocalising the problem and a possible solution, nine times out of ten the answer becomes clear without any input from me. This gives my student more confidence in their own abilities and a real ownership of their thesis, report or paper; after all, they are the expert on that very specific topic. Of course, if my student is going down the wrong path, I will make sure that they are brought back on track.

What this book is not

This book is called 'How to Structure a Thesis, Report or Paper', not 'How to Write a Thesis, Report or Paper' or 'What to Write in a Thesis, Report or Paper'. Don't expect this book to help you with the content of the work, your analytical skills or as a general magic wand to help you get a good grade. This book will help you with the *foundation* of all of that: it will give you the structure on which you can build a thesis, report or paper that shows your abilities off the best. Writing something under each of the sections will go a long way towards helping you pass, but the actual grade you get is <u>your</u> responsibility.

It depends . . .

Ask my students what my favourite two words are, and those who have been awake in class will reply 'it depends' (and probably laugh!). It may seem a little strange that the answer to *every* academic question can be 'it depends', but these two little words will help you to remember, in a class discussion or under pressure in an exam, that there are two (or more) sides to every question. By realising this and including more than one perspective in your answers to your theses, reports and papers – in fact, all exam questions – you will demonstrate to your supervisor and the person grading your work that you understand the world is not simple and clear-cut. It will also help you to realise that the basic structure that this book presents is just that, a *basic* structure; you will have to adapt the structure presented in this book to suit the type of thesis, report or paper that you are writing.

How 'balance' affects your thesis, report or paper

My students often ask me how many pages each section ought to contain. Apart from driving them crazy by saying 'Well, it depends . . .' for the 100th time, I tell them about the 'balance' of their paper. Balance is not something that can be taught, as balance depends on what type of paper you are writing, for whom you are writing the paper, any restrictions on length or content, and in which subject. Balance can only be learned through personal experience, by being aware that it exists and by using your common sense. There are, fortunately, two questions that you can ask yourself that can help you to balance the number of pages you allow for each of the sections in your thesis, report or paper.

The first question is, 'What is the purpose of the thesis, report or paper?' For example, if you are writing a semester paper as part of a methods course, then it is probably a good idea to place more emphasis on the Methodology and Method section of the paper (Chapter 4 in this book), providing lots of detail on your thoughts and considerations about your chosen methodology and method. If, on the other hand, your semester paper is supposed to be practitioner-oriented, then it is probably a good idea to write more in the Reflections section of your paper (Chapter 7 in this book), or maybe even write a completely separate section entitled 'implications for practitioners'. Of course, this means that you will adapt the structure of a semester paper presented in this book to suit your semester paper, but this is not a problem. I'll discuss alternative paper structures more in Chapter 11 of this book.

The second question that you can ask yourself is, 'Where do I show what I can do?' Said in another way, which parts of your thesis, report or paper demonstrate the skills that you have learned throughout the wider degree programme that you are on? This question is more relevant to your final thesis, but it's a good idea to bear it in mind even if you are writing a short semester paper as this will show a breadth of knowledge about the subject of your degree programme. Make sure you answer the questions first, but if you can slip in another concept and justify why it is relevant, don't stop yourself. If you are not sure whether this is a good idea, ask your supervisor.

Follow your intuition

Sometimes, when all else fails, you just have to ask yourself, 'Does this seem right?' and then go with what you think is right. This is part of being critical that is essential to writing an academic piece of work – just applied to the actual structure of your thesis, report or paper. You have got this far as a student, so you already have many of the skills that you need to take you further. It's not necessarily a problem if you get the balance of the thesis, report or paper wrong, just as long as you learn *why* you got it wrong, and that you *don't make the same mistake again.* Never forget that it is up to you to reflect on what went right and what went wrong; this is also valid for the structure of your thesis, report or paper.

Learning aids

Throughout this book, I have included examples of text that will illustrate the points that I am making, and at the end of each chapter, I have included a checklist of the things that you need to consider in order to get the maximum benefit out of this book. The checklist section consists of a number of questions to ask your own supervisor – some 'do's and don'ts' that will all help to improve the structure of your thesis, report or paper and a list of common mistakes that I have seen over and over again during my career as a supervisor. You will find that there are links between the contents of the checklist section in one chapter and the checklist section of another chapter. The implication of this is that when you are reading a chapter in this book, it is a good idea to check back on the checklist sections from the other chapters just to make sure that the links are also clear in your paper.

Text examples

It's one thing to read about how to structure a thesis, report or paper, but a completely different thing to actually see it in practice. Throughout this book, there are examples of text that aim to make the explanation in the book a little bit clearer. These range from a complete example of an Introduction in Chapter 2, to single sentences. All of these have the aim of providing good examples of what a well-structured thesis, report or paper looks like, what to watch out for or ideas on how to structure a particular paragraph in the section.

Checklist: ask your supervisor

When you write a paper, you write it *for* someone. When you are in Higher Education, this is your supervisor and the person grading your thesis, report or paper. This book is developed from the advice that I have given to my students on how to structure their work, so it is clear that if your supervisor wants something written or structured in a different way, then you'd be silly not to follow their wishes. The *Ask Your Supervisor* checklist in each chapter will focus on those aspects of structuring a thesis, report or paper that other supervisors sometimes disagree with me on, or that can be different from subject to subject, or across different types or thesis, report or paper. As a supervisor, it is frustrating to say one thing and have a student do something else, so discuss the points in the *Ask Your Supervisor* checklist with your supervisor so that you both agree on the structure of your thesis, report or paper.

Checklist: do's and don'ts

When you write a thesis, report or paper there are things you can do to make your life easier (which is always nice). The *Do's and Don'ts* checklists are designed to make you aware of the little things along the way that can help you to improve your work. The do's and don'ts are specific to the focus of each chapter rather than things that you can do in general; for example, formatting is a general factor that will be dealt with in Chapter 10 on 'Hygiene Factors', but how to present quotes from those you interview will be discussed in Chapter 6, which focuses on the Findings and Discussion sections of qualitative investigations.

Checklist: common mistakes

I have had the pleasure of supervising several hundred under- and postgraduate students over the last decade when they have written their theses, reports or papers, so I have seen certain mistakes crop up time and time again. The *Common Mistakes* lists will give you the benefit of this experience by pointing out where problems often exist, so you don't make the same mistake. As I say to my students, it's only a mistake if you make it twice.

A generic paper structure

As you will see in the next chapter, it is important to tell the reader of your paper exactly what they are going to encounter in the Introduction, and this book is no different. There is a basic structure to every thesis, report or paper, but there will be differences depending on whether your thesis, report or paper uses qualitative or quantitative methods if you are carrying out an actual investigation and collecting data. This is reflected in Chapter 5 on quantitative investigations, and Chapter 6 on qualitative investigations.

The basic structure of a thesis, report or paper consists of the eight sections below:

1   Introduction (Chapter 2);
2   Literature Overview (Chapter 3);
3   Methodology and Method (Chapter 4);
4   Results (quantitative, Chapter 5) OR Findings (qualitative, Chapter 6);
5   Analysis (quantitative, Chapter 5) OR Discussion (qualitative, Chapter 6);
6   Reflections: Limitations, Implications and Future Research Directions (Chapter 7);
7   Conclusion (Chapter 8);
8   Bibliography (Chapter 9).

The first three sections (Introduction, Literature Overview and Methodology and Method) are common to all theses, reports and papers. After this it is necessary to have slightly different structures according to your data collection method. In the social sciences where I supervise it is common to choose between a quantitative and a qualitative approach to gathering and understanding data, so I have separated the next two sections of the paper (on reporting the results or findings of your investigation, and providing an analysis or discussion of your results or findings in the appropriate context) into individual chapters to make it clearer. The final three chapters (Reflections: Limitations, Implications and Future Research Directions, Conclusion and Bibliography) are once again common to all theses, reports and papers.

Each of these eight sections is further broken down into subsections which are specific to each of the chapters in this book. I find that it is a good idea to write all of the sections and their subsections down in a document before you start writing the body of the text, as with a clear and detailed structure, writing the text will seem like 'filling in the blanks'. As one of my students said to me, as long as you have written something relevant in each of the subsections, you are likely to pass. This is not to say that you *will* pass – remember that this book is about structuring a thesis, report or paper rather than writing a thesis, report or paper – but that the foundation for writing a piece of work that can pass is present.

How to use this book

The fundamental aim of this book is to provide you with a simple yet flexible structure to use when you write a thesis, report or paper. This book will also introduce you to the problems associated with writing a thesis, report or paper, common mistakes, and some tips and tricks to help make your work look, read and – hopefully – grade just that little bit better.

In general, I would advise you to read this book from cover to cover before starting the research and writing process, and then read each chapter again whilst you are writing that particular section of your thesis, report or paper. This will give you advice on how to structure each section individually, with the knowledge in the back of your mind as to how the sections fit together as a coherent whole.

The structure that is outlined in this book is not intended to fit all cases; for example, I haven't provided a structure for a theoretical thesis, report or paper, or a formal literature review, nor have I explained how adopting more complicated approaches to creating and dealing with data, such as grounded theory or mixed methods, has consequences for the structure of your work. As a social science academic of the business school variety, I have written this book primarily with social science and business school students in mind. However, I have tried to make sure that the general idea of a solid structure, irrespective of subject, can help make your life more straightforward. Just leave out the irrelevant sections and use your common sense – and *especially* ask your supervisor. There is a saying: 'listen to all advice and then ignore two-thirds of it' – not following all advice blindly is a useful skill to learn, and where better to learn this than when you are a student with the benefit of a supervisor?

. . . And finally

One thing that I want my students to experience is to be happier when they leave a supervision session with me than when they arrive for a supervision session with me. This might seem a little strange, but think about it this way – the doubts that my student had on their way to the supervision session have been replaced by a feeling of confidence in their own ability to work out the answers to the problem they faced. I would also like you to feel happier when you've finish reading this book – not because it's been boring and you're glad to be done with it, but because you have learned something that is useful and has made you say 'A-ha!' every now and again. And of course, that your thesis or the next report or paper you write will be more straightforward – not necessarily easier, but more straightforward.

Good luck!

The introduction

The Introduction is the first section that you write (it's also the last section that you write, but I'll come back to that at the end of this book). A good way to think about an Introduction is as being the story behind your thesis, report or paper and a road map for reading the rest of your work, with a statement about what you are going to focus on specifically – and what you are *not* going to focus on. The Introduction is therefore very important to get right, as it sets the scene and provides that first impression to your supervisor and the person grading your work. This chapter is one of the longest in this book, and there is a reason for this. Once you have the Introduction written down, you have a reference point that you can go back to throughout the entire research and writing phases of your thesis, report or paper. This will make your life much more straightforward!

An Introduction consists of six elements:

- An 'appetiser';
- The aim of the thesis, report or paper;
- The motivation for the thesis, report or paper;
- The research question;

DOI: 10.4324/9781003334637-2

- The delimitations;
- The structure of the thesis, report or paper.

Each of these elements fulfils a unique role in the Introduction. The appetiser introduces the context of the paper; the aim, motivation and research question focus on the paper itself; and the delimitations and paper structure outline what you are going to include in the paper – and importantly, what you're *not* going to include in your paper.

In this chapter, each of the six elements of the Introduction will be presented in turn, with an example of each. At the end of this chapter, all of the elements will be integrated into one continuous piece of text, so you can read an example of an entire Introduction. The example that I use in this chapter has been created especially for this book and is based on my own research area, political marketing.

The 'appetiser'

The appetiser is the very first part of your thesis, report or paper that your supervisor and the person grading your work will read, and as you know, first impressions are very important. The appetiser sets the scene; it tells a story about the context from which your paper takes its point of departure. The idea is to capture the interest of those who are going to grade your work and make them think, 'Hmm, I'm looking forward to reading this . . .'. Here is an example of an appetiser:

> During the presidency of Donald J. Trump, Trump used his private Twitter account on a daily basis to comment on events in society (Ross and Rivers 2018). By using Twitter as the primary communication channel instead of mass media interactions such as press briefings and interviews,

Trump was able to use short messages, 'tweets', to bypass the traditional role of the mass media as an interpreter and gatekeeper of political messages (Ott 2017). Much has been written about the impact of social media influencers on consumer behaviour (Vrontis *et al.* 2021); could Trump's use of social media to send messages directly to the electorate have influenced voter behaviour, especially those who voted for the first time at the 2020 presidential election?

As you can see, an appetiser starts with the basics: is there any history? What factors are in play? Are there any main characters that are essential to the story? Basically, what is the context? This example of an appetiser is based upon my own research area, but the structure of the example is valid for other areas, especially in the social sciences. Notice that there are references in the appetiser – whilst I would say that most of the Introduction shows how you understand the research area and how you are going to approach the problem, it is good to have references in the appetiser, as the appetiser builds on things that are happening 'in the real world' (these references will be written out in full in Chapter 9). Once you have set the scene in the appetiser, it is time to become much more specific by relating the general research area to your specific question in the 'aim of the paper'.

The aim of the thesis, report or paper

The aim is, simply put, what you intend to achieve by carrying out the research that your thesis, report or paper presents. The aim builds upon the appetiser by making the appetiser more specific – whilst the appetiser provides a general, almost informal introduction to the context of your work, the aim sharpens this to provide a description of the specific area that will be investigated. Here is an example of the aim of a paper:

The aim of this paper is to investigate how political messages on social media affect the voting behaviour of the segment of the electorate who are voting for the first time.

The aim is not the research question. The difference is that the aim is a description of the specific area that you will investigate in your paper, whereas the research question is very specific and phrased as an actual question. You should already be able to see that the Introduction begins by describing the general situation and then becomes specific by focusing the reader on what aspect of the context is important in your thesis, report or paper. In the aim above, we can read that the paper focuses on social media messages, voter behaviour and first-time voters. What it doesn't say is which social media platform we are going to focus on or what type of messages. These will be made specific in the research question and delimitations, which both come after the motivation.

The motivation for your thesis, report or paper

The next element of the Introduction is the motivation. The motivation of your paper justifies the aim and puts the aim back into a wider context. The motivation is narrower than the appetiser, and it is not structured as a story about the past and present, but about how the aim of your research will impact the future. The key question that the motivation answers in the example in this chapter is, "Why is the aim relevant to the paper?" Here is an example of a motivation:

This aim is motivated by a need to understand the impact of social media messages in the political context, as in the commercial context, social media platforms such as Twitter are having an increasingly important influence over the purchase behaviour of young adults (Chen **2015**).

As you can see, I have written 'This aim is motivated by . . .'. The reason for this is that it is very easy to confuse the aim and the motivation, so by being clear that the aim builds on the motivation, it will help you to make a clear distinction between the two. You can also see that I have included a reference to an article in the motivation, as the aim of your paper is what you are going to do, whereas the motivation is the relationship of what you are going to do (the aim) with the wider context (the appetiser). The fourth element of the Introduction, the research question, focuses the appetiser, the aim and the motivation into a single question that guides your research and will be answered in the Conclusion.

The research question

The research question is the most important sentence in your entire thesis, report or paper. This is the question that guides your research and on which you build your work, and this is also the question that you should be able to answer in the Conclusion. The research question should be simple and to the point. Here is an example of a research question in the paper that I am using as an example in this book:

> Therefore, the research question of this paper is:
> 'How does Twitter affect voter behaviour?'
> *Research question RQ1*

When I look at research question RQ1 as a supervisor, there are several words that tell me what to expect when I am reading this paper. I've underlined the words in research question RQ1 that have a special meaning and have implications for this paper. First is the word 'how' – this means that I would expect this paper to focus on uncovering *in what way* voters are affected, and not *if* voter behaviour was affected or not.

The second word that I would focus on is 'Twitter'. The word 'Twitter' instead of 'tweet' signifies that this paper is going to look at Twitter as an organisation or a communication platform, rather than tweets specifically, and I would expect Twitter to be the focus of this paper. I have supervised students who have stated 'Twitter' in their research question and then included a whole section on Instagram in the main body of the text. The number of words that my student used to explain Instagram could have been used in a better way by deleting the section on Instagram and instead using the words to provide more depth in a different section of their work. When I saw that the students had written a section on Instagram, I adopted my normal supervisor behaviour and simply asked, 'If you are writing about Twitter, why is there a section on Instagram?'

The third underlined word in research question RQ1 is 'voter'. This is very broad, as voters can be grouped according to demographics, geography and political affiliation, amongst many, many others. This is where the delimitations come into play – but more on that below. The final word is 'behaviour'. This word means that I would expect this entire paper to be about the *behaviour* of voters, and not, for example, the *attitudes* of voters. In the case of this paper, what voters do, and *not* what voters think.

It is important to be aware of the difference between the aim and the research question. First of all, the aim is phrased as a sentence, whereas the research question is just that – a question. The aim is also more general than the research question. In the example in this chapter, the social media platform that the paper will investigate is not named in the aim, whereas research question RQ1 focuses the reader on the social media platform, in this case Twitter.

A word of warning – it's very easy to try to present several different questions in one research question. This is signalled by words such as 'and' and 'or' in the research question. If you compare research question RQ1 to the following two research questions (RQ2 and RQ3), you'll see what I mean:

Therefore, the research question of this paper is:
'How do Twitter and Instagram affect voter behaviour?'
Research question RQ2

In this case, research question RQ2 is actually made up of two sub-questions – the first sub-question asks about Twitter, and the second sub-question asks about Instagram. If I was looking at a paper based on research question RQ2, I would expect to read about both Twitter *and* Instagram in the example paper, so the paper is in fact *two* papers. Here is another example of a research question that is actually two sub-questions:

Therefore, the research question of this paper is:
'How does Twitter affect voter behaviour, and which voters are most important?'
Research question RQ3

In this case, research question RQ3 is again made up of two sub-questions – I would expect to read about voter behaviour *and* the relative importance of voters, which would require two different investigations. This means that the paper has to include more concepts, and if the paper had a word limit, adopting research question RQ3 will result in a more superficial paper.

A word on secondary research questions. Up until now I have assumed that there will only be one research question in your thesis, report or paper and that the entire work will focus on that one research question. However, some supervisors may want you to write a number of secondary research questions to demonstrate that you are aware of the individual elements of your thesis, report or paper – for example, the important concepts in the literature overview or the appropriate methodology and method. If this is something your supervisor wants you to do, make sure that you add the secondary research questions.

Get the research question right and your life will be much more straightforward than if you make the research question too long, too complicated or too general. This is not to say that a general research question is bad in the beginning of the writing process, as this will give you a good idea about what you are going to investigate without restricting yourself artificially. Restricting yourself by describing a framework where you make it clear what you are going to investigate in your thesis, report or paper, and what you are *not* going to investigate, is written in the delimitations section of the Introduction.

Delimitations

It's important for your supervisor and the person grading your thesis, report or paper to know what you are going to write about; it's just as important for your supervisor and the person grading your work to know what you're *not* going to write about. This is where your delimitations are important. By clearly specifying what you are going to focus on in your thesis, report or paper, you are creating a framework within which your supervisor and the person grading your work have to understand your arguments. They may disagree with your delimitations; for example, they may think that a different theory is more suitable for understanding your research question, but if the person grading your thesis, report or paper is good at their job, they will give you a grade based upon what you have explicitly stated that you will do. This said, if your supervisor asks you to use a particular theory or method and you don't, then don't expect to get a good grade, as you haven't answered the question!

Another reason for being very specific in the delimitations is that your research question can be interpreted in different ways by different people. Compare the following two research questions:

> Therefore, the main research question of this paper is:
> 'How do tweets affect voter behaviour?'
> *Research question RQ4*

> Therefore, the main research question of this paper is:
> 'How do messages on social media platforms affect voters?'
> *Research question RQ5*

Research question RQ4 is adapted from the research question RQ1 at the beginning of this chapter, where 'Twitter' as an organisation or communication platform (RQ1) is replaced with 'tweets' (RQ5) as a communication medium. Research question RQ5 – whilst covering the exact same research topic as research question RQ4 – is much more general and open to interpretation. Both research question RQ4 and research question RQ5 follow the advice that I gave about focusing on one question, but their scope is different. This is why you need to make it very specific as to what you will look at. Here is an example of a delimitations section in the example paper that is suitable for both research question RQ4 and research question RQ5:

> The research in this paper is delimited to one social media platform, Twitter, with the focus on social media messages in the form of tweets from former US President Donald J. Trump's private Twitter account, from the 2016 presidential election until the 2020 presidential election. Whilst we recognise that there are many factors that can influence voter behaviour, and that these influences differ across election contexts, this time frame provides a set of messages that

directly link a first-term incumbent politician to an election. In addition to this, we focus on those members of the electorate who were legally able to vote for the first time at the 2020 presidential election.

There are many different social media, so in this case it is necessary to be specific about *which* social media are being investigated; this is where the delimitations are important. The idea is to start with a relatively broad research question, narrow this down in the delimitations and then use both the research question and delimitations together as a guide when you are researching and writing your thesis, report or paper. Then during the writing process, it will be possible to adjust your delimitations slightly should this be necessary. Adjusting your delimitations whilst you are in the middle of the research process is not something that I would recommend as a normal part of writing a thesis, report or paper, but it helps to check back every now and again whilst you are writing your paper to see whether you are still on the right track.

The structure of your thesis, report or paper

The last section of the Introduction is simply a couple of sentences that detail the structure of your thesis, report or paper. This part of the Introduction is designed to give a very brief overview of what the reader should expect, the road map. It will also help you to structure what comes next. Don't go into great detail when you write about each section; write just enough to give an overview. Here is an example that presents the structure of the paper:

In the following paper, we first provide an overview of our conceptual point of departure, focusing on the specific

factors that are applicable to Twitter as a social media platform relevant to political actors. We then describe our
methodology and method. Following this, we present our
findings and then discuss these findings within the context of the appropriate research. Finally, after reflecting on
the implications for research and practice, we present our
conclusions.

The idea is to provide a simple overview, with no discussion of
the literature, methodology or method that will be used. For
example, it is possible to replace ". . . our conceptual point of
departure . . ." with the name of the theory, concept or model,
and it is possible to replace the next part of that sentence, ". . .
Twitter as a social media platform relevant to political actors
. . .", with something more general. The point is that the sentences that focus on the structure of the example paper provides
the reader with a road map for understanding the logical presentation of that paper.

The complete INTRODUCTION

Finally, here is an example of what I consider to be a complete
Introduction:

During the presidency of Donald J. Trump, Trump used
his private Twitter account on a daily basis to comment on
events in society (Ross and Rivers 2018). By using Twitter as the primary communication channel instead of mass
media interactions such as press briefings and interviews,
Trump was able to use short messages, 'tweets', to bypass
the traditional role of the mass media as an interpreter and
gatekeeper of political messages (Ott 2017). Much has been
written about the impact of social media influencers on

consumer behaviour (Vrontis *et al.* 2021); could Trump's use of social media to send messages directly to the electorate have influenced voter behaviour, especially those who voted for the first time at the 2020 presidential election?

The aim of this paper is to investigate how political messages on social media affect the voting behaviour of the segment of the electorate who are voting for the first time. This aim is motivated by a need to understand the impact of social media messages in the political context, as in the commercial context, social media platforms such as Twitter are having an increasingly important influence over the purchase behaviour of young adults (Chen 2015). Therefore, the research question of this paper is:

How does Twitter affect voter behaviour?

The research in this paper is delimited to one social media platform, Twitter, with the focus on social media messages in the form of tweets from former US President Donald J. Trump's private Twitter account, from the 2016 presidential election until the 2020 presidential election. Whilst we recognise that there are many factors that can influence voter behaviour, and that these influences differ across election contexts, this time frame provides a set of messages that directly link a first-term incumbent politician to an election. In addition, we focus on those members of the electorate who were legally able to vote for the first time at the 2020 presidential election.

In the following paper, we first provide an overview of our conceptual point of departure, focusing on the specific factors that are applicable to Twitter as a social media platform relevant to political actors. We then describe our methodology and method. Following this, we present our findings, and then discuss these findings within the context of the appropriate research. Finally, after reflecting on the implications for research and practice, we present our conclusions.

As you can see, all six of the elements described above are contained within the Introduction, and the Introduction is written in a way that makes it clear *what you are going to do*, *why you are going to do it*, and *how you are going to do it*. Not only does the Introduction provide your supervisor and the person grading your thesis, report or paper a clear thread to follow through the paper, but you can also use it to remind yourself of what you are writing. You will see in later chapters the way in which the Introduction – and especially the research question – are used to make you think about how well the paper is staying on course.

Checklists

Ask your supervisor . . .
> . . . if references are appropriate in the appetiser;
> . . . to discuss the research question with you;
> . . . to make sure that the aim and motivation are different;
> . . . if they want you to write secondary research questions.

Do's and don'ts
- DO write the Introduction first;
- DO remember that the Introduction can be adapted during the research process;
- DO remember that the research question and delimitations are *almost* set in stone;
- DON'T be too specific in the research question – that is what the delimitations are for;
- DON'T create a research question that is actually two sub-questions.

Common mistakes

- The appetiser does not set the scene;
- The aim of the paper is not clear enough;
- The motivation is not relevant to the research question and aim;
- The aim and the motivation are not distinct enough;
- The research question is actually two sub-questions;
- The delimitations are not specific enough – or too specific.

Literature overview

The second section of a thesis, report or paper focuses on presenting the literature that you are going to use. It demonstrates that you have a good knowledge of the subject area, can identify the strengths and weaknesses of the literature that you select, and use the literature to develop hypotheses or justify areas of research interest, depending on the methodology and method you select for your investigation, if you carry one out. Already you can see that the Literature Overview section is going to be integrated within the entire thesis, report or paper – decisions that you make while writing the Literature Overview section have direct implications for decisions about the appropriate methodology and method, what you can find out from any data you collect, and any conclusions that you can draw.

Your supervisor may want the title of this section to be 'Literature' or 'Literature Review', and of course, follow what your supervisor says! Whilst I have no problem if my own students use the 'Literature' title for this section, I do not allow them to use the title 'Literature Review' unless they are writing a very specific type of thesis, report or paper. This is because a 'Literature Review' is a type of academic paper with its own formal method that aims to integrate all of the research on a

DOI: 10.4324/9781003334637-3

particular subject and present the findings as the current state of the research area. I'll discuss the structure of a formal literature review in Chapter 11.

The basic structure of the Literature Overview section of your thesis, report or paper is structured around answering the following five questions:

- Which theory, or model or concept do you use?
- Why do you use this theory, or model or concept?
- What is the theory, or model or concept in the context of your paper?
- Which hypotheses do you derive, or which areas of interest are there?
- How does your Literature Overview relate to your research question?

Which theory, or model or concept do you use?

When a student of mine writes a thesis, report or paper, I ask them to choose <u>one</u> theory OR <u>one</u> model OR <u>one</u> concept to use as the foundation for their work. Notice that I use the word 'or' – your thesis, report or paper needs to be focused, so if there are several theories, or models or concepts, and you are restricted to a limited number of words, then the paper can quickly become superficial. This is valid for all types of papers, from small midterm papers to longer theses. For example, when you focus on one theory, the structure of the Literature Overview section will simply be to present that one theory using the appropriate literature.

Of course, you may want to (or have to) write about two theories, in which case the structure is as follows: first present one theory and relate it to the context, then present the second theory and relate it to the context, and finally demonstrate the similarities and differences between the theories in the context. From this you can see how much extra space it takes to write about two theories.

I've used theories as an example, but the same is valid for models and for concepts. In the case of a theory or model that is made up of multiple concepts, it is necessary to balance the number of words you use to describe each concept in the theory or model so that there is a balance between the concepts. For example, if you decide to use 1,000 words to describe a model with four concepts, you need to use about 250 words on each of the concepts.

What is this theory, or this model or this concept, and why is it relevant to your thesis, report or paper?

After you have chosen the theory, or model or concept that will be the focus of your thesis, report or paper, you need to describe it so that it is clear how you understand the characteristics of the theory, or model or concept. In general, by writing specifically how you understand the theory, or model or concept, you are making the foundation of your work explicit. This in turn means that if you have misunderstood part of the theory, or model or concept, good supervisors will guide you back on the right track, and the person grading your thesis, report or paper will be able to identify where you went wrong and will not let this mistake have too serious an effect on how the rest of the paper is assessed (as long as the rest of the paper is correct, of course!).

An important indicator of the quality of your paper are which references you use in your thesis, report or paper and how they are used to support your understanding of your chosen theory, or model or concept in general and your Literature Overview in particular. For example, if there are only one or two references throughout the entire presentation of a model, you can see that there is unlikely to be a discussion of the positive and negative aspects of the model – the critique – in the context of your research question.

You also need to include other research that has used the theory, or model or concept, as this will give you a good idea about how the theory, or model or concept has been used by other researchers. This is important as you need to have a good explanation for why you use the specific theory, or model or concept that you do. It's not enough to write "this concept is defined as . . ." – you also need to justify this definition. This way, you are providing a reason for your choice and demonstrating its relevance to the aim, motivation and research question. Remember that you don't write *explicitly* how the theory, or model or concept fits with the aim, motivation and research question – this is reserved for the Analysis or Discussion sections, and the Conclusion. Have a look at the following example:

> According to Lees-Marshment (2001a, 2001b), the concept of political market orientation (PMO) focuses on ensuring that the message of the political party (in the case of this paper, via Twitter) follows that of voter markets and thus influences voter behaviour. However, Ormrod (2006) has criticised this conceptualisation of PMO as ignoring the needs of the internal market, that is, party members. As such, by including internal markets in its understanding of PMO, this paper nuances Lees-Marshment's (2001a, 2001b) concept of PMO to focus on markets, rather than voters.

This example is based upon real research articles, and the full references are written out in Chapter 9 of this book. The first sentence provides the understanding of the concept, in this case political market orientation. If you only focused on Lees-Marsh-ment's understanding of the concept, then you would miss out on the critique provided by Ormrod that makes up the second sentence (beginning with "However, . . ."). Finally, missing out the third sentence (beginning with "As such, . . .") would mean that you would not add your own, argued opinion to your the-sis, report or paper. Together, these three sentences demonstrate that you have understood the concept (in sentence 1), under-stood the weaknesses of the concept (in sentence 2), and under-stood how to improve the concept in the context of your own paper (in sentence 3).

A final thing to note is that after the first time the concept is named, 'political market orientation', I have written '(PMO)', and from then on, written 'PMO' instead of 'political market orientation'. This is because I would probably use the name of the concept many times throughout the text, so it makes reading the text quicker just to read 'PMO' rather than 'political market orientation'. It's a matter of balance as to which concepts you abbreviate like this, but a rule of thumb is that it is the central concept of your thesis, report or paper, and it is repeated ten or more times throughout your entire thesis, report or paper. This is also valid for other terms and names of organisations (e.g., 'UN' instead of United Nations, 'BBC' instead of Brit-ish Broadcasting Corporation) and countries ('USA' instead of United States of America, 'PRC' instead of People's Republic of China), amongst many others. If you are unsure, ask your supervisor.

Which hypotheses do you derive, or which areas of interest are there?

Once you have presented the theory, or model or concept, and placed it in the context of your investigation, you need to demonstrate how your research question interacts with the literature. The aim of this is to use the literature to form the basis of hypotheses if you are carrying out quantitative research, or areas of interest if you are carrying out qualitative research. Whilst hypotheses are relatively straightforward to identify and formulate, I have chosen the term 'areas of interest' when discussing research using a qualitative approach, as the term encompasses several different perspectives and is based on the methodology and method that you choose to answer your research question.

Hypotheses

A hypothesis, like the research question, has to be formulated in a very particular way. Whereas the research question is phrased as just that – a question – a hypothesis is phrased as a statement of what is supported by the literature and your interpretation of the literature, in the context of your research question. You state your hypothesis, and then you use your investigation to either say, "Yes, my investigation supports my hypothesis", or "No, my investigation disproves my hypothesis". Of course, it's slightly more complicated than that as there are different ways of creating hypotheses and the relevant terminology (e.g., null hypothesis, alternative hypothesis), so read your methods textbook for an explanation of these. In this book, I will focus on the phrasing of the hypothesis and the common mistakes that students make. Have a look at the following hypothesis:

Hypothesis H_1: There is a statistically significant correlation between Twitter usage and the likelihood of voting.

Example hypothesis H_1

As you can see, this hypothesis can be answered using 'yes' or 'no' – look back to the research question RQ1 in Chapter 2 of this book about the Introduction and you will see that there are links between the way research question RQ1 is written and the way that hypothesis H_1 is written. Reading hypothesis H_1, I would expect to have already read in your thesis, report or paper about Twitter usage and the likelihood of voting in the Literature Overview section, and I would also expect to have read about a justification for there being a correlation between the two, in theory and/or in practice. I would also expect to see at *least* two different questions in the questionnaire, focusing on the level of Twitter usage and on the likelihood of voting.

A key feature of hypothesis H_1 is that it only contains one correlation. Now look at the following hypothesis and see if you can spot the difference:

> Hypothesis H_2: There is a statistically significant correlation between Twitter usage and likelihood of voting or not voting.
>
> *Example hypothesis H_2*

Hypothesis H_2 actually consists of two hypotheses – the first one focuses on the correlation between Twitter usage and likelihood of voting, and the second focuses on Twitter usage and the likelihood of not voting. So, which are you testing? Can you answer hypothesis H_2 with a definitive 'yes' or 'no'? As with the research question for the entire paper, when using a quantitative method, you must only be able to give one answer.

A final note on how you present your hypotheses in the text of your paper – as with the research question, you can make it very obvious what the hypotheses are by adding spaces before and after, just like in this book. I'll come back to the importance of clarity in presenting your text in Chapter 10 on 'Hygiene Factors'.

Areas of interest
In contrast to hypotheses that can be answered using 'yes' or 'no', qualitative investigations often seek to nuance existing

knowledge about a theory, or model or concept, so we are more interested in finding out which ideas and opinions are relevant to the research question that we do not know in advance. For some investigations, there will be one area of interest, covered by the research question of your thesis, report or paper. In others, especially if your thesis, report or paper focuses on a theory or a model with multiple elements, there may be a larger number of areas of interest.

The structure of the Literature Overview when you are identifying areas of interest for a qualitative investigation follows the same general structure as when you are developing hypotheses for a quantitative investigation. First, follow the structure that I introduced above for the presentation and critique of the theory, or model or concept. Then, instead of asking concrete questions, you focus on gaps in how the theory, or model or concept is understood and applied, especially if you are focusing on a novel context. This demonstrates that you 1) understand the theory, or model or concept; 2) understand the context; and 3) understand how the context provides a 'special case' and is able to enrich the theory, or model or concept.

How does the literature overview relate to the research question?

The final element of the Literature Overview is not something that you actually write in your thesis, report or paper itself, but instead it is a question that you ask yourself – how does what you have written in the Literature Overview contribute to answering your research question in the Introduction? In the extreme, you should be able to state why each paragraph in the Literature Overview section is relevant to answering your research question, but my advice is simply to read through the Literature Overview section, all the while thinking about your research question.

If there are any differences between your research question and the content of the Literature Overview section, and you are able to define your own research question, it is necessary to think about what to do. You have three choices: either consider the wording of your research question, rewrite the Literature Overview, or make a note of the difference and wait until later on in the research process to see if anything needs to be changed. I would, however, underline that none of the three options is as good as keeping to your original research question and making sure that the Literature Overview is relevant from the very beginning.

Checklists

Ask your supervisor
. . . to discuss your hypotheses or areas of interest with you;
. . . what they want the Literature Overview section to be called.

Do's and don'ts
- DO check whether your hypotheses can be answered with 'yes' or 'no', if you are carrying out a quantitative investigation;
- DON'T try and cover too much literature – be selective, and if in doubt, narrow your delimitations;
- DO check that what you have written fits with your research question.

Common mistakes
- Choosing more than one theory, or model or concept;
- A hypothesis consists of two hypotheses;
- There is a lack of focus on the appropriate area of interest;
- There is an imbalance between the number of words assigned to the different concepts in a theory or model.

Methodology and method

Two words that often get confused are methodology and method. The two are closely related but are not the same. Basically, your method is *what you do*, and your methodology is part of the wider question of *how you know that you can do what you do*. Your methodology is more complicated and more abstract, and this is why many students leave a discussion of their methodology out of their paper. However, it is just as important to get right and include in your paper as the method, as making your methodology clear shows that you understand why you can investigate what you do. In this chapter, I will discuss both methodology and method, and then continue to focus on the quality criteria you use and the description of the specific process of your empirical investigation.

Throughout this book, I have emphasised how important it is to ask your supervisor what they think and how they want you to structure your thesis, report or paper, as it might be different to the structure that I present in this book. This is especially relevant to the Methodology and Method section, as some supervisors will want you to discuss broader philosophy of science topics in this section, and others still will want you to present a structure that follows a specific research design from your other courses. As always, check with your supervisor!

DOI: 10.4324/9781003334637-4

I will be using a 'bare basics' approach to presenting the process of an investigation that you can use as inspiration for your thesis, report or paper, consisting of a general discussion of your methodology and method. What I won't be doing is discussing what methodology and method are, as you can look at your courses on philosophy of science and/or research methods for this information.

The Methodology and Method section focuses on answering these five questions:

- Which methodology do you use, and why?
- Which method do you use, and why?
- What are your quality criteria, and why?
- How do you carry out the investigation?
- How do these relate to your research question?

Methodology

The methodology is part of a wider understanding of the way knowledge is created and understood, along with ontology and epistemology. I'm not going to discuss what methodology, ontology and epistemology are, as many universities devote entire, obligatory courses to philosophy of science topics, of which methodology, ontology and epistemology are central elements. The important thing in the context of this book is that you need to write a section in your thesis, report or paper about where you stand on questions of knowledge, as this determines how you can treat the information that you get out of those who are participating in the investigation, and also which research questions can be answered.

A very simple example: quantitative and qualitative methodologies are two alternative research strategies for creating and understanding data. Those researchers who use a quantitative methodology understand data as being independent of who is looking at the data. It doesn't matter which person is looking at the data, as the data will be understood in the same way by all people. The assessment of the quality of the data is embedded within the data, not the person who is understanding the data. If you use a questionnaire, for example, you can transform the answers into numbers and the computer will work out your results – you are not involved in this process. These results are then compared to statistical cut-off points, which most researchers can agree on and you can find in statistics textbooks.

Those researchers who use a qualitative research strategy believe that the background and experience of each person determines how the data is understood – ten people can understand the data in ten different ways, and as all ten people have unique backgrounds and experience, the believability of each of their interpretations of the data is dependent on the quality criteria. If you interview a person, for example, and write out the interview transcript, even how you write out the interview transcript has an implication for what you can find – do you include pauses in the transcription, or 'filler' words such as 'er . . .' and 'um . . .'? What does this say about how easy it is for the person you are interviewing to express themselves about the interview topic?

Philosophy of science as a separate section

Sometimes, your university or supervisor will want you to write an entire section in your thesis, report or paper about the philosophy of science approach that you have adopted. This can be as a separate section, where the methodology part of the section is moved to a wider Philosophy of Science section, and the method has its own section. In this case, you will have to use an alternative structure for your thesis, report or paper, like this:

- Introduction
- Literature Overview

- Philosophy of Science
- Method
- Results/Findings
- Analysis/Discussion
- Reflections
- Conclusion

Another way of structuring your thesis, report or paper that emphasises the importance of philosophy of science as a separate element will place the philosophy of science at the beginning of your work, before the Literature Overview. This is to underline that your approach to philosophy of science is important even when deciding which literature to use. In this case, the structure of your thesis, report or paper would look like this:

- Introduction
- Philosophy of Science
- Literature Overview
- Method
- Results/Findings
- Analysis/Discussion
- Reflections
- Conclusion

It will be clear by now that writing about the methodology that you use (and possibly wider philosophy of science topics) is an important part of your paper. Unfortunately, it is also the part of a paper that is most often left out by students because for many, it is difficult to understand. I usually say to my students that if there is an oral defence, it is less likely that they will be asked about the methodology part of the paper and more likely to be asked about the literature section or analysis/discussion, but if they don't write about the methodology (or wider philosophy of science), then they are likely to get asked about it. Of course, your experience in an oral defence may be different; however, talk to your supervisor about how you should include a discussion of your methodology in your thesis, report or paper, even though you are certain of the subject itself.

Method

The method that you use is the practical aspect of your thesis, report or paper – it may be an interview with an expert or a number of consumers, a focus group, a questionnaire, a series of experiments or observations. It is the process by which you carry out the investigation and consists of a discussion of the practical steps that you have taken to find the information that you need to answer the research question. The method is also closely linked to how the methodology affects your interpretation of the data itself. In the following, I will focus on questionnaires as examples of quantitative investigations, and interviews as examples of qualitative investigations. However, you must remember that there are many different ways of gathering information (e.g., experiments, ethnographic studies, focus groups), and that you should make sure to focus on the characteristics of your chosen method of collecting data – remember, this book is about the structure of a thesis, report or paper, not the way the data is actually collected.

When using either a quantitative or a qualitative methodology, you need to state explicitly which method is used (e.g., questionnaire, interview) and how it can help you to answer your research question. Here, you describe the method in general, whereas in the following part of the Methodology and Method section, you describe how the method is applied to your own investigation.

If your research question begins with words like 'Do . . .' or 'To what extent . . .', then you know that you can answer the research question with 'yes/no' or 'small/medium/large', respectively. Of course, it's more complicated than this, but remember the hypotheses that I presented in Chapter 3 of this book on the Literature Overview – you are trying to uncover whether a hypothesis is supported or disproved, so you can check your research question by asking yourself whether you can answer it using yes or no.

If your research question begins with 'How do . . .' or 'Why . . .', then you need to able to answer the research question with various suggestions or a 'Because . . .'. Once more, it is more complicated than this, but remember the areas of interest that I wrote about in Chapter 3 of this book – the idea is to explore the relevance of the theory, or model or concept in order to increase the amount of knowledge using your specific context. You can check your research question by asking yourself if you can answer your research question with a yes or a no. For example, try and answer the following two questions using yes or no:

"Do tweets affect voter behaviour?"

"How do tweets affect voter behaviour?"

The difference between quantitative and qualitative approaches is also an important consideration when you state what role data has in your investigation. At the extreme, are you trying to create a theory, or model or concept, or are you trying to test a theory, or model or concept? These two approaches are called induction and deduction, respectively. For induction, you want to nuance how the theory, or model or concept is understood in your specific context, and for deduction you need to test whether the theory, model or concept is useable in your specific context.

A limitation of these two approaches is that if you adopt an inductive approach, the chances are that you are using a theory, or model or concept that another researcher has already tested using a deductive approach. If you adopt a deductive approach, then it often suffers from the opposite issue – that a theory, or model or concept that you are testing has already been created and expanded using an inductive approach. Both induction and deduction have strengths and weaknesses and are part of a longer process of creating and testing knowledge about theories, models and concepts, labelled the abductive approach, by alternating between nuancing and testing theories, models and concepts.

Your methodology and method are linked as the methodology that you adopt determines which method you use and which research questions you can answer in your thesis, report or paper. The methodology describes your place within a very general philosophical understanding of reality, and the method is how you can understand your research question within your context. In practice, it is often enough to name each element of the methodology and method sections above with a few sentences on what they are and what they mean in the context of your investigation, rather than provide a longer explanation of what they are. Of course, if you are writing a report or a paper for a dedicated philosophy of science course – or if your supervisor says so – then you need to emphasise this section more.

Quality criteria

The quality criteria of your investigation tell the reader how believable your research is. A high-quality investigation will include justifications of all decisions that were made when the data source was selected, along with the way in which the data was created, treated and understood. This is independent of whether your investigation uses a quantitative or qualitative method. A discussion of the quality criteria is often integrated into the discussion of the research process, especially in the case of qualitative investigations where the process of data collection and data interpretation is dependent on one another and cannot be split up – the way you understand the data is personal and determines what you can find. I will only be going through a few examples of quality criteria in this section, so make sure that you check back to your methods textbook to see if other quality criteria are relevant in your thesis, report or paper.

Quantitative methods

In quantitative investigations, the quality criteria are generally straightforward, as their primary focus is on the reliability of the data, the validity of the data and the rules of thumb that govern how the results of statistical outputs are interpreted. Examples of relevant questions that need to be answered to determine the quality of your investigation are: Have you carefully decided which people to ask in your questionnaire? Have you made sure that the selection criteria are explicit? Have you pre-tested the questions and checked the results once the data has been collected for problems, both statistically and with regard to how the questions are understood? Answering questions such as the above and relating them to explicit quality criteria will increase the believability of your investigation. Have a look at the following example, with the important words in **bold** type:

> In order to improve the **content validity** of the questions, I conducted a pre-test amongst a sample of the population. This consisted of asking the respondents to fill out the questionnaire and provide comments to each of the questions about how they understood the question.

There are two sentences in the piece of text above. The first sentence states what sort of quality criteria – in this case, content validity – is being reported on, and the second sentence states how the quality criteria are being ensured in the context of the investigation. This needs to be written for each of the types of quality criteria that you use. My advice is to make a list of all of the quality criteria that you intend to use, and then write each of them using this two-part structure.

In a quantitative investigation, your description of quality criteria and how you addressed them in your investigation are presented in two sections. The first section is part of the Methodology and Method section and describes how you developed the questions for a questionnaire or the process for an experiment – these are usually types of validity. The second section where you write about quality criteria is in the results section, with both validity and reliability statistics being necessary quality criteria, along with comparing your results to the statistical rules of thumb in your methods textbook. I'll go into more depth on the second type of quality criteria in the results section of this book.

Qualitative methods

In qualitative investigations, the quality criteria in the Methodology and Method section of your thesis, report or paper tend to focus more on the process of how you collected, processed and interpreted the data, rather than the data itself. Examples of relevant questions that need to be answered to determine the quality of your research are: Have you documented each stage of the research process? Have you checked your interpretation of the data with the individual you are interviewing or observing, or compared your interpretation of the data with other types of data? Have you acknowledged your own prejudices and positions on the questions that you are asking? As with quantitative investigations, answering questions such as the above and relating them to explicit quality criteria will increase the believability of your investigation. Have a look at the following example, with the important words in **bold** type:

A **member-checking** validity procedure was conducted in order to improve the **credibility** of the data interpretation. This consisted of reviewing the interview transcript with the participants in order to ensure that my interpretation reflected their opinions.

As with the example above for content validity when using a quantitative method, the piece of text consists of two sentences, with the first stating which quality criteria is being reported on (in this case, credibility using a member-checking validity procedure), and the second reporting on how the quality criteria was ensured in practice. You can structure the text in the same way for each of the quality criteria. In qualitative investigations, my advice is to detail all of the quality criteria that you use in the Methodology and Method section, as when you detail your findings in the next section of your paper, the Findings, you are simply reporting what you have found.

Especially in the social sciences, it is more difficult to assess quality criteria when using qualitative methods, as the assessment is based on knowledge, experience and acknowledged opinions rather than a number compared to a rule of thumb. The perceived quality of your paper is dependent on whether you can convince your supervisor and the person grading your thesis, report or paper of your interpretation. This makes it even more important to be explicit about which quality criteria you use and how the quality criteria are suitable for the method.

Alternative types of thesis, report and paper

I consider the two pieces of text above to be the standard that a student should write about quality criteria in their thesis, report or paper, although I realise that some reports and papers are short and so you have fewer words to discuss each of the quality criteria that you use. Here is an example of how a shorter piece of text could be written, using the quantitative example from above:

> Pre-testing the questionnaire increased **content validity** by asking individuals to comment on how they understood each of the questions.

As you can see, the text is much shorter. It doesn't contain as much information as the text above, but it does indicate that you are aware of the importance of quality criteria in general, that you know where each quality criterion is relevant and that you know how to use the quality criteria in the context of your investigation. If you have an oral defence, you may be asked to talk about what the quality criterion is, so be prepared for this. I'll be writing more on oral defences in Chapter 11.

It is a good idea in theses or methods-focused papers to write more information than was given in the text above, as this will demonstrate that you know which quality criteria are relevant, why these quality criteria are relevant and how you ensured the quality criteria in practice. Here is an example of a longer presentation of a quality criterion, again using the quantitative example from above:

> **Content validity** in questionnaire investigations focuses on testing whether each question measures what it is designed to measure (*reference*). In order to improve the **content validity** of the questions, I conducted a pre-test amongst a sample of the population. This consisted of asking the respondents to fill out the questionnaire, and provide comments to each of the questions about how they understood the question.

Now, the text consists of three sentences, with the second and third sentences being the same as in the original example. The new, first sentence provides information about what the quality criterion means in the broader context of a specific method, in this case the content validity of each question in a questionnaire. Notice that there is also a reference (written in *italics*) at the end of the first sentence – this reference is important, as you are using someone else's work (you haven't invented the concept of content validity!). The reference will mostly likely be to the methods textbook that your supervisor recommends, but it must be there.

In my experience, just like the methodology section, many students tend to gloss over the quality criteria that are used to evaluate their investigation, especially if they use qualitative methods. However, I cannot stress enough how important it is to justify how you are going about your investigation and to link this to explicit quality criteria, in order to demonstrate that your investigation is of a high quality – which, of course, it is!

Describing the investigation

The concrete application of the method is a description of what you are going to do and why you are going to do it in the way that you do. In this way, it is similar to the delimitations section from the Introduction, as you are writing down all of the decisions that you make – only when you describe your investigation, the focus will be on what you do, rather than how you delimit yourself to a specific research area.

It is sometimes the case that the description of your investigation and the relevant quality criteria are integrated, as the choices that you make regarding a particular method are dependent on how you ensure the quality of your investigation. This is valid for both quantitative and qualitative investigations. Using the quantitative example from above, I have described part of the investigation in **bold** typeface:

In order to improve the content validity of the questions, I conducted a **pre-test amongst a sample of the**

population. This consisted of **asking the respondents to fill out the questionnaire** and **provide comments to each of the questions about how they understood the question**.

As you can see, the quality criterion (content validity) determines a specific course of action when developing the questionnaire (pre-testing the questions). Other parts of the investigation will not have such a concrete link to any particular quality criteria, so the text will focus exclusively on your decisions and why you made these decisions. Here is an example of describing an investigation, focusing on how a sample was selected:

The sample for the investigation was selected using a snowball sampling procedure, where initial respondents were asked to forward the questionnaire link to those members of their social circle that fitted the inclusion criteria. This allowed the researchers to gain a larger pool of respondents than would otherwise have been possible.

The above text provides a very simple explanation of what was carried out (snowball sampling procedure), how it was carried out (respondents forwarded the questionnaire link) and why (to access a larger pool of respondents). When you describe your investigation in your thesis, report or paper, remember to check whether there is a clear link to the quality criteria, but don't be worried if there isn't a natural link – the most important thing is that you can justify why you have carried out the investigation as you have.

Relationship to your research question

Once you have finished writing your Methodology and Method section, it is important to think about the way in which the section fits with your research question. Just as in the Literature

Overview section, this is a question that you ask yourself rather than a question that you should specifically write down the answer to in your thesis, report or paper. The most important check is whether it is actually possible to answer your research question using the methodology and method that you have chosen, together with whether you are going beyond the delimitations that you stated in the Introduction.

Once you have checked that you can answer your research question using the methodology and method, you can carry out your investigation! Once you have carried out your investigation, you will have data, and you can begin to understand your results or report on your findings, which we will look at in Chapters 5 and 6.

Checklists

Ask your supervisor
- . . . if it is necessary to include a section detailing your methodology;
- . . . how much detail you have to provide on each of the quality criteria.

Do's and don'ts
- DO use the methods textbook your supervisor recommends;
- DO check that the method can answer your research question;
- DO provide a detailed description of your investigation;
- DON'T forget the quality criteria!

Common mistakes
- Not distinguishing between a methodology and a method;
- Not including quality criteria;
- Including the wrong quality criteria;
- Not choosing the right method to answer the research question.

Quantitative investigations

Results and analysis

In this chapter, I will focus on quantitative investigations – that is, the type of investigation that provides (primarily) numerical data. There are many different methods you can use to generate quantitative data, but in this chapter, I will use the example of a questionnaire to explain the structure of the Results and Analysis sections. I have decided to focus one chapter on both the Results and the Analysis sections of your thesis, report or paper, as the two sections form a logical whole – what are your results, and what do your results mean in the context of your investigation?

Once you have carried out your data collection, it is time to present three things: 1) your results, 2) how valid and reliable your results are and 3) whether your hypotheses are supported or rejected. This is followed by your analysis, where you answer the question of what these results mean in the context of your investigation by comparing your results to the literature that you used to develop the hypotheses (in the Literature Overview, Chapter 3). It is here that you demonstrate how good you are at understanding what your investigation actually means in the context of your research question.

DOI: 10.4324/9781003334637-5

In this chapter, we first look at the Results section, which consists of answering the following questions:

- How do you prepare the data?
- What are your data's validity and reliability statistics?
- What are your results?
- Are your hypotheses supported or rejected?

After this, we focus on the Analysis section, which consists of answering the following questions:

- Why are your hypotheses supported or rejected?
- How does this answer your research question?

Results

In previous sections in your thesis, report or paper, you've been through the literature, described and justified your methodology and method, and made sure that the research question is reflected in what you have written up until now and how you have carried out your investigation. Now it is time for what many people consider to be the fun part – finding out what your results are!

Well . . . Sorry to spoil the fun, but there are a couple things you need to do before the *real* fun starts. It is *very* tempting to carry out the statistical procedures you have planned with the aim of finding out whether your hypotheses are supported or rejected, or just seeing what other statistical procedures say about your data, something that I call 'going on a fishing trip'. First of all, you need to prepare the data to make sure that it can be used, and then you need to check the various validity and reliability measures to see how certain you can be of the quality of your results. Then you can calculate the results, and it is only now that you can see whether the hypotheses that you stated in your Literature Overview are supported or rejected.

Data preparation

The first stage is to prepare your data. You will most likely have had lectures on data preparation as part of a methods course, so my first recommendation is, as always, to re-read your notes. Data preparation consists of necessary things such as looking for, and dealing with, missing data; checking for descriptive statistics such as means, standard deviations, skewness and kurtosis; and generally making sure that your data can actually be used with the statistical procedures that you have selected. You may have to transform the data in some way, or standardise the data if this is required by your chosen statistical process.

I'm not going to discuss what you need to do or why you need to do it, as this is what you can find in the methods textbook that is recommended by your supervisor. The reason why I am emphasising data preparation is to save you time. If you do start to calculate the results with data that is not prepared, then you will have to go back and carry out all of the calculations again. If you have six months to write a thesis, this may not be too much of a problem, but with a deadline of four weeks for researching and writing an entire paper, you can see how a day used on playing with unprepared data could be better used on something else.

Validity and reliability

Once you have followed your methods textbook on data preparation, dealt with issues such as missing data and checked the descriptive statistics, it is time to look at the validity and reliability measures. In the quality criteria section of the Methodology and Method section, I wrote that the quality criteria for quantitative investigations is split up into two stages. The first stage is when you develop the processes you will be using to collect the data; the example that I used focused on the ability of the questions in the questionnaire to measure what you want them to measure, known as content validity. The second stage, described in the Results section, occurs once you have collected all of the data from your investigation and is usually carried out by comparing your results to a set of statistics or measures that provide 'rules of thumb'.

'Rules of thumb' are generally agreed numerical boundaries that measure characteristics of your data. These numerical boundaries can be found in the methods textbook that your supervisor recommends. At the most general, we can talk about validity and reliability. Validity focuses on the extent to which the data actually measures what it is supposed to measure – if a question asks about the behaviour of an individual, is the question phrased in a way that actually measures the behaviour of that individual? Reliability, on the other hand, focuses on whether the question would measure the same thing if it were asked to another member of the population that was not included in the investigation's sample – would the question be understood in the same way?

A concrete example: If you drive too fast in a car, you may be caught by a speed camera. In the context of this book, it provides a good example of validity and reliability. The photograph from a static speed camera is considered by the police to be **valid**, as a speed camera is designed to measure how fast a car is travelling by comparing the position of the car against lines on the road in two photographs that are taken a given time apart, and the speed camera is accepted as successfully measuring this speed. However, there are always environmental or mechanical factors that cannot be controlled for, so the ability of the camera to **reliably** measure the same speed twice is less than perfect – this is why there is usually a margin of error (for example, 3%).

Are your hypotheses supported or rejected?

Now it is time for the fun part, finding out whether your hypotheses are supported or rejected. In the majority of theses, reports and papers, this is simply a case of going through each of the hypotheses, stating what each hypothesis was and showing, through the use of the computer output, that the hypothesis was supported or rejected. There is a philosophical reason for writing 'supported' rather than 'proved' – you have tested the hypothesis in one context, so you cannot say whether the hypothesis will also be valid in another context. Therefore, you can only provide more support for the hypothesis, you can never prove it. Look at your notes from your philosophy of science or research methods course, or ask your supervisor.

Analysis

In the Results section of your thesis, report or paper, you will have identified whether each of your hypotheses has been supported or rejected. The main question that you need to answer in the Analysis section of your thesis, report or paper is: do the hypotheses follow or contradict the literature that you presented in the Literature Overview section? At the end of the Analysis section, you will also be able to provide a concrete answer to the research question.

Do the hypotheses support or reject the literature?

The most important question to answer is whether each hypothesis supports or rejects the literature. In the Results section, you did not include any references to other literature, and instead focused on the results and whether they supported or rejected each hypothesis. The opposite is true in the Analysis section – each of the hypotheses was developed to test an aspect of an existing theory, model or concept, so in the Analysis section you must take the same articles you used in the Literature Overview and discuss whether the conclusions of the articles are supported or not. Here is a fictional example of this way of structuring a text:

> Vrontis *et al.*'s (2021) research argued that non-company influencers often have a higher impact on consumer behaviour than standard marketing activities carried out by companies. However, our results demonstrate that this is not the case with political parties (H_3: p> .05). The reason for this could be that the politics is different, and so 'standard' marketing models of consumer behaviour cannot be used without careful adaptation.
>
> (Ormrod *et al.* 2013)

This way of structuring the text is as follows: the first sentence focuses on what the articles stated (from the Literature Overview), the second sentence focuses on whether the hypothesis was supported or rejected (from the Results section) and the third sentence focuses on your interpretation and what the results mean for the articles from the Literature Overview.

Answering the research question

At the end of the previous chapters, I have advised you to think about whether what you have written fits with your research question. Up until now, this has just been a question for yourself, as it should be clear from the text of your thesis, report or paper what the link is to the research question without having to spell this out. However, at the end of the Analysis section, you have all of the information that you need in order to provide a concrete answer to your research question. You have been through the literature, described and justified your methodology and method and presented the results and how these results can be analysed in the context of the literature. Now you can answer your research question.

My advice is to answer your research question under a subtitle, for example, 'Summary'. Using a subtitle makes it clear that what you are writing is not part of the analysis of the results, but instead you are providing a short summary of your analysis. This can be laid out in a similar way to the Conclusion section, just without the description of the structure that you used in order to get to the answer. Here is an example of a summary of a quantitative investigation:

SUMMARY

The results of the empirical investigation support Hypothesis H_1, that voters do pay attention to Twitter when deciding which candidate to vote for, and for Hypothesis H_2, that Twitter is seen as a legitimate alternative news source to the traditional mass media. These results indicate that Ott's (2017) research into Twitter as a competing information source can be used in the context of this paper. However, the results reject Hypothesis H_3, that non-candidate influencers affect voter behaviour, which goes against current research (e.g., Vrontis *et al.* 2021). As such, the answer to the research question is that tweets do affect voter behaviour, but only directly, in that the impact of influencers over voter behaviour is insignificant compared to influencers' impact on consumer behaviour in the commercial context.

The first sentence in this fictitious example restates the results of the investigation, that hypotheses H_1 and H_2 were supported. The second sentence applies the literature (Ott 2017) to the results of hypotheses H_1 and H_2. The third sentence integrates the result of hypothesis H_3 with the impact on the literature (Vrontis *et al.* 2021). The final sentence provides an explicit answer to the research question as briefly as possible.

Alternative section titles and thesis, report or paper structure

I advise my students to use a structure that separates the Results and Analysis sections, as it gives them a straightforward way of dividing their paper up into what the computer output is and whether their hypotheses are supported or rejected in the Results section (without references), and their interpretation of the computer output in the context of the literature in the Analysis section (with references). However, all supervisors are different, and your supervisor may want you to use alternative titles for each of the sections. For example, your supervisor may want you to call the Results section 'Results and Analysis' and the Analysis section 'Discussion'. Another variation is to call the Results section 'Results' and the 'Analysis' section 'Analysis and Discussion'. In both cases, you must follow your supervisor's advice.

These two alternative section structures provide you with a clue as to what information each section contains simply by their titles. If your supervisor wants you to have two sections with the titles 'Results and Analysis' and 'Discussion', then you know that the first section needs to be structured as what the results are, whether each hypothesis is supported or rejected and what it means to the theory, model or concept, with the second section focusing instead on what the results mean in the wider context, where all hypotheses are taken as one result. The second alternative structure, with separate sections for 'Results' and for 'Analysis and Discussion', needs to be structured in a similar way to the structure I have been through in the main part of this chapter, but with an obvious division between the analysis of each hypothesis and the discussion of all of the hypotheses as a whole. Again, if you are not sure, ask your supervisor!

Checklist

Ask your supervisor
. . . what the Results and Analysis sections should be called;
. . . how much detail you should provide in the Results
section.

Do's and don'ts
- DO prepare your data;
- DO check the validity and reliability statistics;
- DO answer the research question;
- DO include references in the Analysis section;
- DON'T include references in the Results section;
- DON'T waste time by 'going on a fishing trip'

Common mistakes
- Using irrelevant statistical procedures;
- Introducing references into the Analysis section that do not
appear in the Literature Overview section;
- Beginning to write the Analysis as part in the Results section;
- Mixing up validity and reliability.

Qualitative investigations

Findings and discussion

Investigations using a qualitative methodology, such as interviews, focus groups and observational studies, are commonly used in the social sciences to uncover what people think and feel, or how they behave, in a particular context. Because of this, you have to interpret the data yourself, which brings with it questions of the quality of the investigation and of your own interpretation of what you have found. This chapter covers two sections in your thesis, report or paper that you include if you are carrying out an investigation using a qualitative methodology, namely the Findings section and the Discussion section.

Whereas the distinction between Results and Analysis in papers adopting a quantitative methodology is easily identified, this is not the case with investigations that adopt a qualitative methodology. To start with, it is not possible to distinguish between reporting what you have found and analysing what you have found, as you are coloured by your own perspective. What you find is determined by your analysis of what you regard as important. You then discuss what you have found in the Discussion section, where you compare what you have found to what other researchers have found or argued for.

DOI: 10.4324/9781003334637-6

This is why I choose to call the sections 'Findings' and 'Discussion'. Of course, your supervisor may disagree and call the sections 'Findings and Analysis' and 'Discussion', or 'Findings' and 'Analysis and Discussion', and you must always follow your supervisor's advice! In this chapter, we first look at the Findings section, which consists of the following questions:

- What have you found out?
- Which quotes exemplify your arguments?
- How do your findings relate to your research question?

After this, we focus on the Discussion section, which consists of the following questions:

- What do your findings mean in the context of the literature?
- How does your discussion of your findings answer your research question?

Findings

The findings section focuses on just that – what you have found in your investigation. It is different from the Results section that I described in Chapter 5, as Results are numerical and are (usually) what the computer calculates from the data, whereas Findings are how you interpret the data – the difference is that by choosing what is important from the qualitative data, you are already analysing the data before you have gotten anything out of it. This data can be in the form of written text (e.g., interview transcripts, tweets, websites, company reports), or images or recordings (e.g., adverts, YouTube videos, your own recordings), and there are many different ways of extracting your findings. Look at your methods book for the alternative methods available to you.

Quotes

If you are carrying out interviews or focus groups in your investigation, it is often possible to record the session, usually on a sound file. This means that you will be able to write out a transcript of the sound file and use direct quotes from the participants. You need to ask for written permission to record the sessions first, and you need to make sure that any legal requirements (e.g., GDPR, non-disclosure agreements) are fulfilled. It is very important to ask your supervisor about the rules for this, as not following the rules can have serious consequences.

Back to the transcription – there are many ways of transcribing data, so check with your methods textbook and decide which transcription method is most suitable to your investigation, and remember to be specific about why your way is the appropriate way (see Chapter 4). If you can use direct quotes from the participants of the interviews or the focus group, it is a good idea to put these quotes into the main text of the paper. This will help you to justify your arguments, and support the quality of your research.

Here is an example of how I would write a direct quote in the Findings section:

"I use Twitter a lot to get political information"
Participant A-3, 04:56

There are two things to notice here. First of all, the quote itself is centred and there is a double line break between the text above and the quote. This makes it very clear to the reader exactly what the quote is. You could write the quote as part of the normal text and this would be fine, but it is a good idea to make it very clear which piece of text is the quote. Most theses, reports and papers have limits defined in words or pages of a standard length, so it doesn't matter if you have too many actual pages.

Quotes do take up a lot of space when they are written out as I have done here, but there is a reason for it.

The second thing to notice is the reference for the quote. It consists of three pieces of information about the quote. The first piece of information is the label of the participant who gave you the quote, in the above case Participant A. The second piece of information is the quote number from the participant, in the above case quote number 3 – that is, this is the third quote that you have used in your findings section from Participant A. By numbering all of the quotes in this way, you will be able to refer back to each quote individually in the text if you need to.

The quote number from the individual participant (in the above example, the third quote) can also provide you with some information when writing your thesis, report or paper. You may find that a certain participant is providing you with some really good quotes, but by only choosing quotes from one participant, you aren't using all of the perspectives that the different participants have given you. If you find that one participant has given you 20 quotes, and the other participants have given you 10 in total, you can easily see that you need to go back and think carefully about whether your findings are representative of all of the participants, or only representative of one participant.

The third piece of information is the time stamp, in the above case four minutes and 56 seconds into the recording. You may not be able to submit a sound file of the recording with your thesis, report or paper, but you may be able to submit a written transcript instead – just replace the time stamp with a line number (or even page and line number) in order to make it obvious where in the transcript the quote appears. This will help you keep track of where each of the quotes are, and it will also make it easier for the person grading your work to look up the quote in the context of the individual interview to see whether they agree with your interpretation or not.

If you are using images, it can often be a good idea to put these images in your thesis, report or paper itself. This allows you to refer to the images in the text; this will help the person grading your work to understand your interpretation of the data and see whether they agree with your interpretation or not. Use the same system of referring to the image as I have explained when referring to quotes from a transcript. This way, it will make it easier for you to identify exactly which image you are writing about.

One piece of advice I give my students is to not include references to other research in the Findings section. The Findings section consists of *your* findings in *your* investigation, so including the findings of other researchers means that they are contributing to what you are finding, which is not the case. Not including references to other work in the Findings section will also make it obvious to you what your findings are, and what the discussion of your findings is in the context of the literature.

Discussion

Whilst the Findings are what you have found in your investigation, the Discussion focuses on what you have found in the context of the wider literature that you included in the Literature Overview section of your thesis, report or paper (Chapter 3 in this book). As I've written above, the Findings section should contain no references to other research, whereas the Discussion section should contain many of the references that you used in the Literature Overview section.

I advise my students to only use the references in the Discussion that have also been used in the Literature Overview – that is, no new references. This restriction is also valid for the quotes that are used in the Findings section – in the Discussion, you must only refer to quotes that have already been presented in the right context in the Findings section. In that way, there is a clear link between the Literature Overview section, Findings section and the Discussion section, and you can demonstrate that you are focusing on answering the research question.

It is in the Discussion section that you demonstrate to your supervisor how good you are at taking what you have found yourself and reported in the Findings, and understanding it in the context described in the Literature Overview section. I would advise against using quotes in the Discussion, as quotes demonstrate what you have found, whereas the Discussion focuses on what the quotes mean. Remember that you have given each quote a unique reference in the Findings section, so it is easy to refer back to the quote if you need to. Have a look at the text below for a fictional example:

Vrontis *et al.*'s (2021) research argued that non-company influencers often have a higher impact on consumer behaviour than standard marketing activities carried out by companies. However, our interview participants saw the influencers as being politically active themselves (Participant A-2) and so "tainted" through their association with a particular political party (Participant C-5). The reason for this could be that the politics are different, so 'standard' marketing models of consumer behaviour cannot be used without careful adaptation. (Ormrod *et al.* 2013)

This text has the same structure as the example in the analysis section of Chapter 5, but with the difference that the second sentence is changed to reflect the different methodology, method and research question. The second sentence contains two references to quotes that are in the Findings section. The first interview reference is simply to the second quote by Participant A, whereas the second interview reference (Participant C-5) also uses a word from the quote, 'tainted'. This is fine as the word 'tainted' is very specific and uncommon – a word like 'good' is much more general and common, and is used in many different ways, so it does not have the same specific meaning.

As for a general structure to the Discussion section, this depends on your method. If you are conducting a thematic analysis of a written text, for example, then you could arrange the Discussion section according to each of the themes in turn, demonstrating how they interact with the literature, and then finish the Discussion section with a summary that links the themes together and answers the research question. An alternative would be to discuss all of the themes at the same time, comparing the themes to one another as you write. Of course, you may find that another structure works better. The important thing to remember is that the discussion (and all of the other sections) must be in a logical order. What do you think is the right order?

Answering the research question

The final part of your Discussion should focus on making sure that you answer your research question. This can follow the same structure that I presented in Chapter 5 on the Results and Analysis, by writing a dedicated 'Summary' to the Discussion section. Here is an example of such a summary:

SUMMARY

The findings of the empirical investigation underlined that the participants did pay attention to Twitter when deciding which candidate to vote for, and that Twitter was seen as a legitimate alternative news source to the traditional mass media, supporting Ott's (2017) research into Twitter as a competing information source. However, non-candidate influencers were not seen as relevant by most of the participants, going against current research (e.g., Vrontis *et al.* 2021). As such, the findings of this paper indicate that tweets do affect the voting behaviour of the participants in the investigation, but only directly, in that the impact of influencers over their voting behaviour may not be as pronounced as is the case in consumer behaviour.

The text is almost the same as the summary text in Chapter 5, but the wording is changed to reflect the methodology, method and research question, as well as the fact that it is not possible to generalise across all voters, but instead represent a deeper understanding of how an individual voter is affected.

Checklists

Ask your supervisor
   . . . what the two sections should be called;
   . . . how your quotes should be presented;
   . . . how much detail you should provide in the Findings section.

Do's and don'ts
* DO include quotes in the Findings section;
* DO answer the research question;
* DON'T include references in the Findings section;
* DON'T worry if you have a lot of pages – quotes take up a lot of space.

Common mistakes
* Writing the Discussion section as part of the Findings section;
* Not making quotes clear in the text;
* Using complete quotes in the Discussion section (individual words are fine if they are very specific).

Reflections

Implications, limitations and suggested future research directions

When I defended my PhD thesis, one of my examiners said, "Thank you for your presentation. So what?" I was completely confused; it was clear to me what the implications of my PhD were. That was just it – I had spent three years writing my PhD, and I was so deep into the subject that I didn't realise that what was clear to me might not be clear to someone else. I survived the defence and was awarded my PhD, but the experience of mild confusion bordering on devastation has remained with me since. From that day on, I have told my students what happened in my PhD defence, and I have asked them in our supervision sessions to answer the 'So what?' question – and it has helped many of them.

So how can you avoid this problem? It's actually rather easy – just put yourself in the position of the person grading your thesis, report or paper, and try and make sure that you have spelled out clearly what the implications of your work are, both for the individuals who have provided the data for your work and for the relevant institutions and organisations in the wider society. There are also limitations – some parts of your research undoubtably didn't go quite according to plan. Finally, there are suggestions for future research and practice – if you could do the research project again, what would you do differently?

DOI: 10.4324/9781003334637-7

The reason for the Reflections section is to make sure that the person grading your thesis, report or paper can see that you are aware of your own weaknesses *and that you can learn from them*. Learning from your mistakes is an important skill, both now and in the future, as making mistakes and learning from them is a good way of improving for the next time you have to write a thesis, report or paper. The Reflections section consists of answering the following five questions, which are linked:

- What are the implications of your research for academics?
- What are the implications of your research for practitioners?
- What are the limitations of your research?
- What are your suggestions for future research?
- How do the implications and limitations relate to your research question?

What are the implications of your research?

You have carried out a piece of research, so it's important to explicitly state what the implications of your research are for other academics, if they want to replicate what you researched in your thesis, report or paper. It might seem a bit of a long way from your research in a semester paper to a five-year academic study involving hundreds of respondents, but the point is to demonstrate that you can identify the consequences of what your research has found out. If you have found out that a concept can be understood in different ways by different people, then researchers may pick up on this and look again at the way the concept is understood. Well done, you've just contributed to academic research!

It's also important to explicitly state the implications for practitioners, especially if you have an academic background in business studies, or if you are writing an internship paper or consultancy report that is naturally focused on providing specific solutions to real-world problems. If you are reporting back to an organisation that helped you with access to data or their employees, it is necessary to write a short report to show your appreciation, and this part of the Reflections section can form the basis of that short report.

What are the limitations of your research?

Every piece of research has limitations. Sometimes, things don't go the way that you planned; you might not have been able to get as many respondents to your questionnaire as you wanted, the interviews may not have gone as well as you'd hoped or, in retrospect, it might have been more appropriate to focus on fewer issues than you did in your research question by having more specific delimitations in the Introduction. It's important to spell out these limitations in your thesis, report or paper so that the person grading your work can see that you acknowledge what went wrong. If you know what went wrong, this is actually a strength – it means that you won't (or you shouldn't!) make the same mistake again. The question is, how would you do things differently if you could carry out the research again?

Suggested future research

Remember the delimitations in the Introduction (Chapter 2)? In the delimitations, you stated what you were not going to look at and made the focus of your paper very clear. Now you have to state what you would do in the future if you could carry out your research again, or if you were to give another academic some advice on how they can replicate your research. There are two directions you can focus on. The first direction is expanding on what you did not do, which is a logical extension of the delimitations in the Introduction. The second direction is based on your investigation; maybe one of your results didn't quite fit with what you expected, or you had a surprising finding in the light of previous research. In both of these cases, you can write that future research could investigate your results or findings further.

Linking implications, limitations and future research

Answering the research question is the basic aim of your thesis, report or paper, so it is important to link the research question to all three elements of the Reflections section – the limitations, implications and suggested future research. With regard to the limitations, what couldn't you answer? Did you manage to carry out the entire investigation as planned, or were there some issues that meant that part of the research question was not answered? What about the implications for practitioners and research?

The three elements of the Reflections section naturally fit together. Starting with the implications, you are stating what the findings or results of your thesis, report or paper mean for the actors who are involved in the investigation or in the wider context, and for researchers who wish to replicate your investigation. You are also making clear how future research can use what you have discovered to answer the new questions that have arisen as a result of your investigation. There are, of course, limitations, although these limitations, whilst based on what went wrong and affecting what you cannot say to practitioners and researchers, can be put right by future research.

This is where you can write all three elements together to one, logical paragraph. It goes something like this: 'An implication is *this*, a limitation is *that*, but the limitation can be solved by doing *these things*'. Here is a more concrete example of what

I mean, with the important words in **bold** typeface. It is a fictional example, but it serves to illustrate the point:

> One **implication** for political managers of this research is that Twitter is good at communicating short messages to first-time voters. However, a **limitation** of this research is that it focuses specifically on Twitter, so we cannot examine the impact of longer, text-based messages (for example, on Facebook) or visual messages (for example, on Instagram and YouTube). **Future research** could expand the scope of the investigation to include other social media platforms and other types of messages.

This is the structure of the Reflections section of your thesis, report or paper – you choose the most important implications from your Analysis or Discussion, and then demonstrate how the implications are limited and that addressing these limitations can form the basis of future research. You can repeat the structure as many times as you need to, but try and make the number of implications realistic – don't try and squeeze three implications out of your Analysis or Discussion when there are only really two that are important. You may have only a small number of words left to use, so which implications you choose are important.

A word on references in the Reflections section – sometimes it is possible, or even a good idea, to include references in your Reflections section as part of the future research element. For example, you could emphasise that one researcher's understanding of a theory, or model or concept is more suitable in your context than how another researcher understands the theory, or model or concept, and you could support this emphasis by giving examples of relevant references. However, I would recommend that you only use references that you have already used in the Literature Overview, as this keeps the paper one 'whole'.

Summary

The *Reflections: Implications, Limitations and Future Research* section of your paper is made up of three elements which are linked together. The purpose of the Reflections section is to demonstrate that you can provide concrete recommendations for practitioners and researchers (the implications), identify any problems that you had and how these problems affect the recommendations that you can give to practitioners and researchers (the limitations), and how the problems can be addressed in future research (the future research element).

Checklists

Ask your supervisor
   . . . if there should be references in the Reflections section;
   . . . how many implications you should include.

Do's and don'ts
* DO integrate the implications, limitations and future research elements of the Reflections section;
* DO accept that there are limitations to your work;
* DO link the limitations in the Reflections section with the *de*limitations in the Introduction;
* DON'T worry if some things didn't go according to plan in your research – reflecting on these is an important skill.

Common mistakes
* Not making the implications of your research clear;
* Not acknowledging the limitations of your research;
* Not demonstrating how your research can contribute to the direction of future research.

The conclusion – and the introduction revisited

The last section in your paper is the Conclusion. It is here that you provide an overview of what you have done, how you have done it and what you have discovered. A rule of thumb is that it should be possible for you to read the Introduction and the Conclusion, and from this gain all of the knowledge that you need to understand the paper. However, the Conclusion is much more than simply a summary of the previous sections; it is in the Conclusion that you make sure that the person grading your thesis, report or paper knows that you have answered the research question. The Conclusion consists of answering the following questions:

- What was the research question?
- How did you answer the research question?
- What is the answer to the research question?

Once you have written the Conclusion, your thesis, report or paper is almost finished. I say almost finished, as whilst you have a completed first draft that can be submitted if you run out of time, I would advise rereading your work and checking on whether what you have written in the Introduction still fits with

DOI: 10.4324/9781003334637-8

what you have written in the body of the text in the Literature Overview section and Methodology and Method section.

The conclusion

A good way to start the Conclusion is to state your research question again. This can be written as something along the lines of:

The research question that was asked in this paper was:

How does Twitter affect voter behaviour?

Simple, right? You copy the research question that you made explicit in the Introduction and paste it into the sentence above. If you want to make it even clearer as to what your research question is, you can format the research question the same way as you did in the Introduction – a double line break, then the research question, then another double line break and on with the text. This means that from the beginning of the Conclusion, the person grading your thesis, report or paper knows what they are going to grade you on. Of course, if the person grading your work has set the question themselves, then this will be obvious to them, so it is more so that you remember the question that you were actually supposed to answer. Either way, repeating the research question is a great way to start the Conclusion.

The sentences that follow the repetition of the research question deal with the overarching structure of your thesis, report or paper – that is, how you went about answering the research question. In the following example, I have used the 'Findings' and 'Discussion' from Chapter 6 on qualitative investigations; if you have conducted a quantitative investigation (Chapter 5), you can simply replace 'Findings' with 'Results', and 'Discussion' with 'Analysis', together with checking on the methodology and method.

This example of a Conclusion takes its point of departure in a paper, and can be written like this:

> In order to answer the research question, this paper began with an overview of the literature on voter behaviour and the impact of social media in the political sphere, with Twitter as the focal social media platform. This was followed by a presentation of the social constructivist methodology and interview method, and subsequently the findings of the investigation. After this, the paper discussed the findings of the investigation in the context of the literature on voter behaviour, and drew implications for practitioners and for future research.

By this point, you should have noticed that the Introduction and the Conclusion are very similar; the Introduction provides a road map of what you're going to do, and the Conclusion reminds the person grading your thesis, report or paper of how you have gotten to where you are now. The easiest way of writing this part of the Conclusion is to look at the 'structure description' element in the Introduction and rewrite it to focus on what you have done. This will give you the first paragraph of the Conclusion.

The next paragraph draws on your Results or Findings, and your Analysis or Discussion (depending on whether you have used a quantitative or qualitative methodology, respectively). If you have lots of words left to use on the Conclusion, then you can write a paragraph for each of the sections, but in most cases, you will only have a single paragraph. Here is a fictional example of how you can write this paragraph, assuming that you used a qualitative methodology:

> The findings of the investigation demonstrate that voters do pay attention to Twitter when deciding which candidate

to vote for, and that Twitter is seen as a legitimate alternative news source to the traditional mass media, which supports Ott's (2017) research into Twitter as a competing information source. However, non-candidate influencers were not seen as relevant, going against current research (e.g., Vrontis *et al.* 2021). As such, the conclusion of this paper is that Twitter does affect voter behaviour, but only directly, as the impact of influencers over voter behaviour may not be as pronounced as is the case with consumer behaviour.

The text above consists of three sentences. The first sentence reports on the first finding (legitimacy of Twitter as a news source) and continues to state how the finding fits with the existing literature from the Discussion (Ott's 2017 research). The second sentence follows the same structure, with the Findings (that influencers are not relevant) followed by the Discussion (Vrontis *et al.* 2021). The final sentence sums up the research by answering the research question. You can check by replacing the word 'conclusion' with 'answer to the research question'. If you can do this and the sentence still makes sense, then you have answered the research question. Well done!

The introduction revisited

Yes, you read the title correctly: the first section that you write is also the last section that you write – or rather, *adjust* – so that your thesis, report or paper becomes one, cohesive whole. This may seem a bit odd, but if you understand your thesis, report or paper as a journey, you'll realise that sometimes where you end up is not exactly where you thought you would end up when you started. Research is, in many cases, an evolutionary process;

whilst you still end up at generally the same destination (a finished, well-structured thesis, report or paper), the route that you take may deviate *slightly* underway – there may be a better way to reach the destination. So how do you adjust your Introduction to make your thesis, report or paper into one, cohesive whole?

First, you need to read through your thesis, report or paper again. The first time that you read through your work, you will most likely find some formatting, spelling and grammar mistakes (I did when I was writing this book!). I will deal with these in more depth in Chapter 10 on Hygiene Factors, but you can correct the text for these language mistakes whilst you are reading your thesis, report or paper through at this point, if you find that it works better for you.

When you read through your almost-finished thesis, report or paper for the first time, constantly ask yourself whether what you are reading fits with the research question. In the extreme, you should be able to choose any paragraph from your thesis, report or paper and be able to explain how that paragraph contributes to answering the research question. The next stage is to read through each section independently and ask yourself whether the section fits with the other sections. For example, if you are reading through the Literature Overview in the context of a qualitative investigation, think about how the theory, or model or concept that you have used, together with the areas of interest that you have identified, affect the structure of the Findings section – are the Findings structured according to the theory, or model or concept, or the areas of interest, or is there another reason for structuring the Findings as you do?

It is this constant attention to your thesis, report or paper *as a whole* that will mean that your work is understood *as a whole*, and not as several individual sections. This, in turn, will mean that your arguments are clear and the paper reads in a more professional way. Here is an example of what I consider to be a complete Conclusion:

CONCLUSION

The research question that was asked in this paper was:

How does Twitter affect voter behaviour?

In order to answer the research question, this paper began with an overview of the literature on voter behaviour and the impact of social media in the political sphere, with Twitter as the focal social media platform. This was followed by a presentation of the social constructivist methodology and interview method, and subsequently the findings of the investigation. After this, the paper discussed the findings of the investigation in the context of the literature on voter behaviour, and drew implications for practitioners and for future research.

The findings of the investigation demonstrate that voters do pay attention to Twitter when deciding which candidate to vote for, and that Twitter is seen as a legitimate alternative news source to the traditional mass media, which supports Ott's (2017) research into Twitter as a competing information source. However, non-candidate influencers were not seen as relevant, going against current research (e.g., Vrontis *et al.* 2021). As such, the conclusion of this paper is that Twitter does affect voter behaviour, but only directly, in that the impact of influencers over voter behaviour may not be as pronounced as is the case with consumer behaviour.

Checklists

Ask your supervisor
. . . if you have any doubts!

Do's and don'ts
- DO read through your thesis, report or paper again once you have finished writing the Conclusion;
- DO constantly question how what you have written contributes to answering the research question;
- DON'T assume that you can't change the Introduction;
- DON'T be afraid to rewrite some text, if you think that it is necessary.

Common mistakes
- Not thinking of your thesis, report or paper as one, whole document;
- Not leaving time at the end of the writing process to check the above.

References and the bibliography

For theses, and most reports and papers, it is necessary to use references. These references can be from many sources, such as peer-reviewed academic journals, books, newspapers and websites. Finding good references takes practice, but it is also something that your library can help with. The relevance of a reference is generally determined by the topic of your thesis, report or paper, and more specifically, by your research question – what central words are there in your research question, and are they central to the reference?

When it comes to how many references you need in your thesis, report or paper, again it is a case of balance. What are you writing – an internship report of 15 pages, or a thesis of 100 pages? Is your thesis, report or paper focused on answering an abstract research question, or a practical research question? Who are you writing the paper for – a practitioner, a generalist or an academic expert in the field? There are not many external references in this book, as it is based upon my own professional experience, so I use references as examples. However, if you read one of my academic articles, you will see that I use many more references to back up my arguments.

DOI: 10.4324/9781003334637-9

Once you have found possible references, it's time to evaluate their quality. Sometimes, this is relatively straightforward – if the reference in question is an article from a peer-reviewed academic journal, then you are on pretty safe ground. There are, of course, exceptions, but as a general rule of thumb, you can safely use academic articles that are relevant to your research question.

The same goes for books written by researchers and published by companies that specialise in academic books. You do have to be a bit more careful here, as sometimes books are written to present a new theory or approach to a research area and are thus generally appropriate, whereas others are written in order to start a debate and might not be appropriate to your thesis, report or paper. Use your intuition and common sense, and don't forget that the relevance of a reference depends on your research question.

The next type of reference is not academic but can still be relevant. Traditional newspapers, trade magazines and other mass media sources can also be used in your thesis, report or paper, but you have to be more careful. These sources can provide you with contextual information for your research. The important question that you need to ask yourself is, *what is the purpose of including this reference?* If the reason is to support an academic argument, you need to be careful, whereas if the reason is to focus the reader of your paper on the context of your research question, then you are generally on safer ground.

The last type of reference is openly editable wikis, online blogs or forum posts. The most well-known openly editable wiki, *Wikipedia*, is an important source of knowledge, but because it can be edited by anyone, I don't recommend it as a reference for academic knowledge. The same goes for blog posts and forum posts; these are generally sources of opinions about a topic rather than rigorous, peer-reviewed academic work. Of course, the blog posts and forum posts can be written by academics or other highly respected professionals in their fields, so again you have to decide whether or not to use the reference based on your intuition and common sense.

A final word on the general subject of references – plagiarism. Plagiarism is a very serious offence in higher education, as it involves taking someone else's research and using it as your own – copying, basically. If you use someone else's research, ALWAYS reference them. If in doubt, reference the other person's research one too many times rather than one too few. This is also valid for your *own* previous work – self-plagiarism is also a serious offence in higher education. All educational institutions have sophisticated computer programs that search for pieces of text across the world, even amongst papers that have been submitted by students at other higher education institutions. Each educational institution has its own policy for plagiarism; the <u>minimum</u> penalty at my university was the cancelling of the paper, and the maximum was a five-year suspension from <u>all</u> universities in Denmark. I cannot stress it enough: if in doubt, ask your supervisor!

The bibliography

In my experience, the Bibliography is one of the sections in theses, reports and papers that does not get enough attention. This can be a problem, as some people who grade theses, reports and papers will immediately look at the Bibliography to get an idea of which references have been used, so a well-formatted Bibliography will create a good first impression. As we all know, good first impressions are important!

When presenting your references in the Bibliography, use a referencing system such as those standardised by *Harvard University*, the *American Psychological Association* or the

Chicago Manual of Style. You need to ask your supervisor about their preference – some supervisors (like me) don't mind which system a student uses as long as a system is used, whereas other supervisors do have a preference for one system over another.

The references in the text are closely linked to the references in the Bibliography in a formatting sense, as the most important thing to remember is that your supervisor and the person grading your thesis, report or paper can find the reference for themselves. So, if you can't find the specific reference, just make sure that you have put as much information as you can. After all, you found it, so your supervisor and the person grading your thesis, report or paper will also be able to find it and judge for themselves whether the reference is suitable.

Below is the list of the references that I have used in this book. I haven't used any particular referencing style on purpose, as this list is just to demonstrate that sometimes it is not a problem as long as you can find the reference (you can check this for yourself):

Chen, H. (2015), "College-Aged Young Consumers' Interpretation of Twitter and Marketing Information on Twitter", *Young Consumers,* Vol. 16 (2): 208–221.

Lees-Marshment, J. (2001a), "The Marriage of Politics and Marketing", *Political Studies,* Vol. 49 (4): 692–713.

Lees-Marshment, J. (2001b), *Political Marketing and British Political Parties: The Party's Just Begun.* Manchester: Manchester University Press.

Ormrod, R. P. (2006), "A Critique of the Lees-Marshment Market-Oriented Party Model", *Politics,* Vol. 26 (2): 110–118.

Ormrod, R. P., Henneberg, S. C. and O'Shaughnessy, N. J. (2013), *Political Marketing: Theory and Concepts.* London: Sage.

O'Shaughnessy, N. J. (1990), *The Phenomenon of Political Marketing.* London: MacMillan.

Ott, B. L. (2017), "The Age of Twitter: Donald Trump and the Politics of Debasement", *Critical Studies in Media Communication*, Vol. 34 (1): 59–68.

Ross, A. S. and Rivers, D. J. (2018), "Discursive Deflection: Accusations of 'Fake News' and the Spread of Mis- and Disinformation in the Tweets of President Trump", *Social Media + Society*, Vol. 4 (2).

Vrontis, D., Makrides, A., Christofi, M. and Thrassou, A. (2021), "Social Media Influencer Marketing: A Systematic Review, Integrative Framework and Future Research Agenda", *International Journal of Consumer Studies*, Vol. 45 (4): 617–644.

There are a number of important things to note. First of all, the references are in alphabetical order. This makes it easier for your supervisor and the person grading your thesis, report or paper to find the references in the Bibliography. The second thing to note is that the Bibliography is not divided up into different types of reference – books (Ormrod *et al.* 2013) and articles (Ott 2017; Vrontis *et al.* 2021) are not separate but are part of one list. The third thing to note is that there are no 'secondary' references – that is, references that are not used in the text but you still consider to be important; if the reference is important enough to go in the Bibliography, it is important enough to go in the text. Finally, the two references from Lees-Marshment are both from 2001, so you need to distinguish between the two – different referencing styles have different ways of doing this, so make sure that you are aware of this when you prepare your Bibliography.

Other issues can arise when formatting the references in your thesis, report or paper. First of all, you may find a reference in an academic article to a second academic article, which looks as if it could contribute a lot to your own thesis, report or paper. Here, it is necessary to go to that second academic article, so you can check that the second academic article does say something that is relevant. However, you may not be able to find that second academic article, so here it is necessary to indicate that you think that the second academic article is important by referencing it in the text and in the Bibliography, but also that you have not been able to find the second academic article. You can do this by using the word 'in' and the academic article in which you found the reference to the second academic article. Here is an example of how you can do this:

O'Shaughnessy (1990, in Ormrod *et al.* 2013)

From a practical perspective, using a specific referencing system will also make your life more straightforward, as by going through your thesis, report or paper and reading every line will force you to check for inconsistencies, spelling and grammar mistakes and other issues that you might not otherwise have noticed. Simply paying attention to the Bibliography will make your thesis, report or paper seem more professional. These are both what I call 'aesthetic hygiene factors', which I will discuss in Chapter 10. If in doubt, check the Bibliography of an academic article to see how it is done.

Checklists

Ask your supervisor
- ... if you are in doubt (or look at the Bibliography of an academic article);
- ... which referencing system to use (e.g., Harvard, APA);
- ... how many references are appropriate.

Do's and don'ts
- DO use peer-reviewed, academic articles;
- DO use books or edited book chapters written by researchers;

- DO use company websites and reports – but only if they are relevant;
- DO use newspapers and magazines – but only if they are relevant;
- DON'T use openly editable wikis, blogs or forum posts as academic sources;
- DON'T plagiarise or self-plagiarise!

Common mistakes
- More is *usually* better, but consider what type of work you are writing and whether the references are included in any restrictions on the number of words;
- Not paying enough attention to the Bibliography.

Hygiene factors

A good friend of mine once looked through a draft of an article that I had written and commented that I had to add a few more references to a key researcher as a 'hygiene factor'. What my friend meant by this is that some things *just have to be* in the thesis, report or paper you are writing. These things can vary from referencing key researchers in your subject to acknowledge their contribution over time (my friend's observation), to something as simple as formatting your thesis, report or paper in a particular font or layout; they don't necessarily add anything to your grade, but it might subtract from your grade if these hygiene factors are not taken into consideration.

Most hygiene factors focus on general layout, formatting, spelling and grammar, along with making sure that your thesis, report or paper reads in an accessible way and that the text looks professional and 'pleasing to the eye'. Making sure that you pay attention to these aesthetic hygiene factors also means that it is easier for your supervisor and the person grading your thesis, report or paper to understand your arguments. Your supervisor and the person grading your work can then focus on how your research contributed to your conclusions and how you answered your research question, rather than trying to work out what you

DOI: 10.4324/9781003334637-10

have written. These aesthetic hygiene factors are more import-ant than many give them credit for, so don't forget them!

Making sure that the aesthetic hygiene factors are appropriate to your thesis, report or paper is a key consideration, as how aesthetic hygiene factors affect your work depends very much on what type of work you are writing (e.g., an academic thesis, a report for practitioners) and who you are writing for (e.g., your supervisor, a company). There are certain things you can do to improve the language, accessibility and general profes-sional appearance of your thesis, report or paper. This will help to create a positive atmosphere around your work, as for your supervisor, and especially for the person grading your work, it is frustrating to have to navigate through a thesis, report or paper and struggle to follow your arguments.

Formatting

Formatting consists of laying out your thesis, report or paper in a way so that it visually looks professional. There are many elements to a visually professional thesis, report or paper, includ-ing appropriate margins, line-spacing, font and text alignment. The first thing you need to check is whether your supervisor has some guidelines for laying out a paper – some educational institutions have rules for margin width or specify a certain font, and some supervisors also have a preference. Normally, I am very pragmatic when it comes to formatting, but I do ask my students to align the text of their papers in a justified way, with lines of text reaching both margins.

Fonts

If you have the freedom to choose which font you use, then think very carefully about your choice. Times New Roman is a common font, as is Calibri, but you may prefer a different font. It's not a problem to use your own preferred font, but think about whether it makes your thesis, report or paper easier to read. If it does, then you can use the font. If it doesn't, then it might be a good idea to choose a different font. Here are some examples of the research question in different fonts, all at the same size, with the name of the font in brackets after the research question:

How does Twitter affect voter behaviour? (Times New Roman)
How does Twitter affect voter behaviour? (Baskerville)
How does Twitter affect voter behaviour? (Calibri)
How does Twitter affect voter behaviour? (Edwardian script)

Of the four fonts above, the first two, Times New Roman and Baskerville, are serif fonts. A serif font has small ornamental additions at the end of the letters and can seem more traditional and serious. A sans serif font, like Calibri, does not have these additions, has a more 'block-like', modern appearance and can seem more relaxed and informal. If you look at the logos of different brands, you will see that some use a serif font, and some use a sans serif font. Which you use is up to you (or your supervisor), but it is important to consider the font as a way of presenting your thesis, report or paper. I have included the fourth font, Edwardian Script, as an extreme example of a serif font – you can clearly see that it is not suitable as a font when you are writing a thesis, report or paper.

Figures, diagrams and tables

Another thing to check is that all figures, diagrams and tables have a title and a number. This is necessary so that the reader knows what they are looking at – what does the figure, diagram or table represent? Which figure, diagram or table is the text referring to? In a thesis, report or paper with one figure, diagram or table, it is not too much of a problem if you forget to write the number of the table, but if you are using several images to illustrate your findings, or several tables with the results for different validity or reliability statistics, you can see that it is a problem if your supervisor and the person grading your thesis, report or paper cannot quickly and easily find which figure, diagram or table they need to look at in order to find the information that you are referring to in the text.

'I' or 'we'?

Look at any academic article and you will see that the authors refer to themselves as 'we'. This is also the case when there is only one author. So, the question is, which do you use? Using 'I' is more informal and can be used when you are writing reports or papers for a non-academic audience, or an academic audience with whom you want to create a relaxed connection (like I am using in this book). Using 'we', on the other hand, is more formal and best used in theses, reports and papers where you have to distance yourself and your own opinions from the arguments and conclusions of your work. A last alternative is to simply go through the paper and reformulate each sentence where 'I' or 'we' occurs to either 'the author' or 'the authors'. Ask your supervisor for their opinion, as different supervisors have different preferences regarding how you refer to yourself in a thesis, report or paper.

Formatting references

References also have to be formatted. You may have access to automatic referencing programs, such as Endnote, which can make your life easier, as you can set the referencing style to a particular system and then let the computer do the rest of the work. An alternative is to do it yourself; this is the way that I work, as I find that I like to check the references in the text. First, I go through the text and check that all of the references that I have used in the text are referenced in the Bibliography. Then, I go through all of the references in the Bibliography to check that they are in the text. In this way, you can be certain to catch any stray references that were put in at the start of the writing process but that you didn't use in the end, for whatever reason.

Language, spelling and grammar

After you have finished writing your thesis, report or paper and you have made sure that the question you have answered in the Conclusion is the same as the question that you asked in the Introduction, it is time to check your paper for language – silly spelling and grammar mistakes, and the overall readability of your work.

You may be thinking, 'Why is he writing about readability now? Surely it would be better to tell me about that at the beginning of the writing process?' The answer to this last question is, again, it depends – everyone has their own writing style, so it is important not to limit yourself by artificially writing in a certain way. There may be some sentences where you know that you could use a better word, but you just can't think of it. In this case, keep on writing and then come back to the sentence later on.

I used this system myself when I was writing this book. For example, I wasn't sure how to format the titles of the sections throughout the book (e.g., Introduction, Methodology and Method, Conclusion). Should they be in bold face? Should they be in italics? You can see what I ended up with, and this was after I had talked to my editor and looked at the formal requirements of the publisher – in your case, your supervisor – but whilst I was writing, I didn't think about this question.

In general, I say to my students that they should just write until they cannot write any more, and then go back and see which pieces of text are too long, which are too short, and whether there is an imbalance in the number of words used in each section of their thesis, report or paper. Some people write a lot – I am guilty of this myself – so I just let myself write and then go back to shorten the text. If you finish writing and there is too little text, you need to read through what you have written and think about whether certain sections are not treated in enough depth. It may be obvious which sections are too short, or you can go back to the questions at the beginning of each of the chapters in this book to see whether you have answered them properly.

It also depends on what sort of thesis, report or paper you are writing. If you are writing a postgraduate thesis with a large investigation, you have to include elements from all of the stages in the structure, and my advice would be to put more weight on those areas of the thesis that can show a general understanding of *all* of the relevant courses on your degree programme. In a thesis, you can prioritise the Literature Overview and the Results and Analysis sections, or Findings and Discussion sections, depending on your methodology and method. If, on the other hand, you are writing an internship report, you need to prioritise the implications part of the Reflections section, as that is the point of the internship report. Finally, in a methods paper, you need to prioritise the Methodology and Method section and the Results or Findings section. Think about what the purpose of your work is, and prioritise accordingly.

The second stage consists of reading your thesis, report or paper out loud, making sure that you focus on saying each word. Read the text in the triangle below:

Figure 10.1 *Top-down processing*

Paris in the Spring, right? Wrong. Read the text in the triangle again, this time out loud. The sentence in the triangle is actually 'Paris in <u>the the</u> Spring'. Did you spot the extra 'the'? If this is the first time that you have been confronted with this, then you probably didn't notice the extra 'the'. This effect is caused by your brain using what cognitive psychologists call 'top-down processing' in order to quickly reach an answer; your brain uses previous knowledge about a sentence in order to speed up the reading process. Basically, the brain is lazy and takes as many shortcuts as possible in order to avoid doing work (sound familiar?). In the context of your thesis, report or paper, it means that sometimes extra words will creep into or out of sentences without your consciousness being aware of it. If you just read the text in your head, you might not catch this sort of mistake.

A second issue is spelling. Read the text below:

> If you can raed tihs txet tehn you are nmarol, as yuor biran jsut lkoos at the frsit and lsat lterets in ecah of the wdros and tehn raenarergs tehm besad on psat enxcepreie. Not eyrenove can raed it so I've witrten a 'traslonirtan' at the end of tihs pgae.

You've probably seen text like this on a social media site, and it proves my point about the mind being tricked in another way. Once more, the ability to read text that is misspelled is caused by your brain being lazy. In this case, you can understand what your brain is doing as a type of 'predictive text', like that found on smartphones. The difference is that you usually get it right (and the smartphone sometimes gets it wrong with very funny results), but when proofreading your paper, this is not always a good thing. Here is the text as it should be written:

> If you can read this text, then you are normal, as your brain just looks at the first and last letters in each of the words and then rearranges them based on past experience. Not everyone can read it, so I've written a 'translation' at the end of this page.

I know that it is often not possible, but if it is possible, don't look at your thesis, report or paper for a few days once you've finished it to give your mind a rest so you can look at your thesis, report or paper again with fresh eyes. If it is not possible, then my advice is to take an afternoon and evening off – go for a long walk with someone, work out, go to the cinema – *anything* that takes your mind off of your thesis, report or paper, even for a short while.

When you read your paper the next day, you'll have fresh eyes and will spot some mistakes (I do!). If possible, read your thesis, report or paper out loud to a friend or partner; if neither of these is available, even a plant or the wall is enough. I guarantee you that there will be small mistakes, even a double space, so if you are able to build time into your writing process to check your thesis, report or paper through, it is a good idea to do so.

Checklists

Ask your supervisor
  . . . about their preferences with regard to the different formatting options;
  . . . what style you need to adopt, if you are uncertain.

Do's and don'ts

- DO just write, you can always return to the text and change it;
- DO read your thesis, report or paper out loud, as it will help you catch any silly mistakes;
- DO think about who you are writing the thesis, report or paper for, and for which course.

Common mistakes

- Prioritising the wrong section;
- Not correcting spelling, grammar and formatting mistakes.

Alternative thesis, report and paper structures, and the oral defence

Experience has shown me that the vast majority of my students have carried out an investigation in the real world and have either developed a questionnaire or conducted a number of interviews. For this reason, this book has focused on two ways to structure a thesis, report or paper based on whether you are using one of these two methods in your investigation. Of course, there are several other types of theses, reports or papers that you will either be asked to write by your supervisor, or that you choose to write yourself. The first part of this chapter deals with three alternative types of theses, reports and papers and demonstrates how the structure that I've presented in this book can still be used, albeit adjusted, to reflect the unique characteristics of each type of thesis, report or paper.

The second part of this chapter looks at the oral defence (or viva in the case of some theses). Some students get worried about their oral defences, but it doesn't have to be this way. Whilst the oral defence is technically not part of the written thesis, report or paper, in some cases it is part of the exam, and you can actually

DOI: 10.4324/9781003334637-11

use some of the structure of your thesis, report or paper to structure your answer. I've included some tips in this chapter that can help you to use an oral defence to your advantage.

Alternative types of theses, reports and papers

My general advice is that all theses, reports and papers need to include the elements of each of the sections that I have covered in this book. However, there may be some theses, reports and papers that you write that have a different structure – whether this is decided by your supervisor, the course design or if you decide to do something differently. In these cases, it is still important to think about and use the structure that is presented in this book, but only use the sections that are relevant to your thesis, report or paper. In the following, I will go into more depth with three alternative structures for a thesis, report or paper: the first alternative structure focuses on understanding a case, the second changes the content of the structure presented in this book, and the third puts the structure in a different order to that which this book focuses on.

If you are writing a thesis, report or paper that compares and contrasts alternative perspectives on a case using data that existed at that point in time, you might not need to go out and collect any primary data yourself. In this case, the Literature Overview section will contain a description of the alternative perspectives that you are going to use, and why these perspectives help you to answer your research question; the Methodology and Method section will focus on the case study method, and the strengths and weaknesses of this method; the Findings section will focus on how the case can be understood using the alternative perspectives that you have presented in the Literature Overview section; and the Discussion section will compare and contrast the alternative perspectives (with the Reflections and Conclusion afterwards). As you can see, this structure is basically the same as the structure that has been presented in this book, it just focuses on describing the case study method and its strengths and weaknesses.

When you write a formal literature review, you don't go out and ask people questions or interview them about why they think what they do. Instead, a formal literature review involves searching for academic articles and books on a very specific issue and then understanding how they fit together. This is a rather simplified description, as there are also different literature review methods, some that follow a quantitative approach to selecting articles and books (e.g., the selection criteria is the presence of a chosen keyword) or qualitative approach to selecting articles and books (e.g., the selection criteria is the informed opinion of the researcher).

Whilst a formal literature review follows the general structure presented in this book, the questions you need to ask yourself are slightly different. For example, in a formal literature review, it is often a good idea to have a dedicated section after the Introduction that introduces the background to your thesis, report or paper. Your Results – the number of articles and books that you select during your search process – can possibly be included in the Methodology and Method section.

My basic advice is to use your intuition and think about what is logical. One possibility is to change the title of the Methodology and Method section to something that describes the content of the section better – for example, Literature Selection. As the literature is selected, then you can go straight to the Literature Review section of your thesis, report or paper. Ask your supervisor whether they have a preference. For a formal literature review, a structure could be like this:

1   Introduction
2   Background

3 Literature Selection
4 Literature Review
5 Reflections: Implications, Limitations and Future Research
6 Conclusion

Finally, a grounded theory approach to research turns the structure presented in this book around. In a nutshell, grounded theory takes its point of departure in the creation of theory from observations. It should be no surprise that this implies that the Methodology and Method section needs to come before the Literature Overview section, as the literature on the subject is part of the data that you select – the results of previous research can provide one perspective on your research question, but it is usually necessary to include your own observations. For a thesis, report or paper that uses a grounded theory approach, the structure would be like this:

1 Introduction
2 Methodology and Method
3 Findings
4 Discussion
5 Implications, Limitations and Future Research
6 Conclusion

Each of the sections would be structured as described in the relevant sections in this book, it would just be the order that is changed. It will also keep you aware that Literature Overview is considered to be Findings rather than a dedicated Literature Overview section in itself. Of course, it may be necessary to expand on the Introduction to make sure that the context is explained in enough depth (appetiser, aim and motivation), and you will have to think carefully about the Delimitations, as the point of grounded theory is to expand knowledge, making detailed Delimitations counterproductive.

The overarching advice is, don't take the structure presented in this book as given. Sometimes it will be necessary to change the order that the sections come in, sometimes other section titles may be more appropriate. Use your intuition and your common sense; ask yourself what is most logical in relation to the content of the section, the relationship of the section to the whole and the type of thesis, report or paper that you are writing. And, of course, ask your supervisor for their opinion – they have seen many theses, reports and papers and can help you to use the most appropriate structure.

The oral defence

For your thesis and some of your reports and papers, you will undoubtably have the good fortune to have an oral defence, where you sit opposite your supervisor and maybe an external examiner and are grilled on what you have spent the last couple of months working on. Yes, that's right, an oral defence is a good thing. An oral defence gives you the opportunity to explain any mistakes, clear up any uncertainties that your examiners may have and demonstrate that you can take your work one step further. You can also use it to create a framework within which the discussion can take place, which gives you an advantage. So, embrace the oral defence, as it may move you up a grade.

This is, of course, easier said than done. Many of us, including me, have 'gone cold' in an oral exam. I know from personal experience that it is really not nice to face your supervisor and an external examiner and not be able to answer questions about the thesis, report or paper that you have worked on for the past few months. It's also not nice for your supervisor and the external examiner when a student goes cold in an oral defence, as supervisors are sometimes faced with a student who has attended class every week, was always well-prepared and active, but falls at the last hurdle.

The first thing to remember is to be prepared. Make sure that you ask your supervisor what their expectations are, and check the formal requirements in the course description – if you have to make a presentation, make sure that you know how long you have for it. It's no good having a detailed presentation that will take you 20 minutes to go through if you've only got five minutes to present. If possible, make sure you know exactly when the exam takes place and where the exam room is; if you can have a look inside the exam room, all the better, as you will know more about what to expect on the day.

If you are allowed a presentation, you can use it for three things: going through the elements of your thesis, report or paper; pointing out any weaknesses or mistakes that you have noticed after you submitted your work; and building on the conclusions of your work. When you go through your paper in the presentation, you need to remember that the person grading your thesis, report or paper *has actually read your work*. This means that they have a good idea about the structure and content of your paper, so you don't need to use the entire presentation going through what you have done – you can safely assume that they know this. This said, you do need to use *some* time presenting what you have done; a rule of thumb is two-thirds of the presentation.

A second use for the presentation in the oral exam is to acknowledge any mistakes that you made in your thesis, report or paper. I don't mean spelling or grammar mistakes, but mistakes in the content of your thesis, report or paper; in your arguments; or in the calculations that you have presented in your work. Don't worry about being embarrassed about making mistakes, and definitely don't hope that the person grading your thesis, report or paper didn't catch the issue. The fact that you are able to look at what you have done and see the weaknesses means that you have understood your own work at a higher level.

A third use for the presentation is to give 'something more'. By this I mean some more information that is not contained in your thesis, report or paper but builds upon the conclusions of your work. The context may have changed for the organisation that you worked with; what has happened, why has this happened and what impact does it have on your conclusions? If you have focused on an issue in your Reflections section, use the presentation to discuss your thoughts further. This addition to your presentation fulfils two purposes. Firstly, it demonstrates that you can do more than just write a thesis, report or paper; you have actually understood what your conclusions mean. Secondly, it means that you can create the framework for the discussion in the oral exam.

When you have finished with your presentation, you will generally be asked some questions based on your work. Some of these questions will naturally focus on what you have written; maybe the person grading your thesis, report or paper is unsure of something and wants to clear it up, or maybe they want to hear your opinion about an issue that relates to the conclusion of your work or that you have brought up in your presentation. The most important thing to remember is that the person who is grading your thesis, report or paper is genuinely interested in entering into a dialogue with you about what you have written. After all, you are the person in the exam room who knows most about your thesis, report or paper, right?

You can actually use the structure in this book to answer questions that are asked by the person grading your thesis, report or paper. Think of the questions that the person grading your thesis, report or paper asks as being the research question; you then state which model, or theory or concept from your work you will use to answer their question, after which you provide your analysis or discussion, and then conclude with the answer to the examiner's question.

Checklists

Ask your supervisor
. . . which structure is most appropriate;
. . . to help you prepare for the oral defence, if there is one.

Do's and don'ts
- DO remember that the structure presented in this book is a general structure – your thesis, report or paper may be in a different order;
- DO give 'something extra' in the oral defence presentation, if you have one – remember, the person grading your work has already read your paper;
- DO think about how you want to use each of the slides in the presentation at the oral defence;
- DON'T panic at the oral defence! Remember, you know the most about your thesis, report or paper.

Common mistakes
- Not thinking about which structure suits the type of thesis, report or paper;
- Not preparing for the oral defence.

How to structure a thesis, report or paper

This chapter provides you with a complete overview of each of the sections and their respective questions. If my students are new to writing a thesis, report or paper, I advise them to write out each of the questions in a fresh document, then answer them all. After that, the text can be written together, and there should be enough in each section to answer the research question. Try it the next time that you write a thesis, report or paper.

1. Introduction

- The 'appetiser': what is the context of your thesis, report or paper?
- What is the aim of your thesis, report or paper?
- What is the motivation for your thesis, report or paper?
- What is the research question?
- What are the delimitations of your thesis, report or paper?
- What is the structure of your thesis, report or paper?

DOI: 10.4324/9781003334637-12

2. Literature overview

- Which theory, or model or concept do you use?
- Why do you use this theory, or this model or this concept?
- What is the theory, or model or concept?
- What is the theory, or model or concept in the context of your thesis, report or paper?
- Which hypotheses do you derive, or which areas of interest are there?
- How does your Literature Overview contribute to answering your research question?

3. Methodology and method

- Which methodology do you use, and why?
- Which method do you use, and why?
- What are your quality criteria, and why?
- How do you carry out the investigation?
- How do these relate to your research question?

4. Quantitative: results

- How do you prepare the data?
- What are your data's validity and reliability statistics?
- What are your results?
- Are your hypotheses supported or rejected?
- How does this relate to your research question?

5. Quantitative: analysis

- Why are your hypotheses supported or rejected?
- How does this answer your research question?

OR

4. Qualitative: findings

- What are your findings?
- Use quotes to exemplify your arguments.
- How do your findings relate to your research question?

5. Qualitative: discussion

- What do your findings mean?
- How do your findings answer your research question?

6. Reflections: implications, limitations and suggested future research

- What are the implications of your research for practitioners?
- What are the implications of your research for academics?
- What are the limitations of your research?
- What are your suggestions for future research?
- How does this relate to your research question?

7. Conclusion

- What was the research question?
- How did you answer the research question?
- What is the answer to the research question?

8. Bibliography

- Which referencing style do you use?
- Are all of the references in the text also in the Bibliography?
- Are all of the references in the Bibliography also in the text?
- Are all of the references in alphabetical order?

Finished! Sort of . . .

After more than a decade of supervising students at various levels, I asked my students whether my presentation of the template in Chapter 12 and the advice that I gave them in a seminar series was something that they thought other students would benefit from. The answer was a resounding 'yes', and after encouragement from even more students, I wrote this book in order to help you structure a thesis, report or paper. The idea is that when you have a structure, you can 'fill out the blanks', which will make your life more straightforward – not necessarily easier, but more straightforward.

The structure that I have presented in this book is generic, and whilst it is valid in many instances, sometimes you will need to adjust the structure slightly, either to fit the type of thesis, report or paper you are writing or to follow the wishes of your supervisor. This structure is also based on a social science paper with a real-world investigation, and I primarily use questionnaires and interviews as concrete examples. However, you may study something in the arts or natural sciences, so you will need to think about what suits your field of study best. It's a case of 'listen to all advice, and then ignore two-thirds of it'.

DOI: 10.4324/9781003334637-13

Often, you will be given a title for a report or paper that you then have to answer; other times, it is up to you to decide on the title. If you do have to decide on your own title, it needs to be done with care, as it is the very first impression that you make. Likewise, you may be asked to write an abstract and some keywords, and if you are writing together with an external organisation, you may have offered that organisation a short report on what you have found. This is more difficult if there are two or more organisations involved in your study, but it is possible.

When all is said and done, it is the wishes of your supervisor that are the most important guidelines to follow, as each supervisor has their own preferences. Some supervisors prefer what I call the 'Findings' section to be called something else, like 'Findings and Analysis' or 'Analysis'. Others prefer the Methodology and Method section to be before the Literature Overview section. Some are even specific about which referencing style to use. I cannot stress it enough – <u>always follow your supervisor's advice</u>!

Title

With many exam papers, you are given a title that you then answer. However, if you are able to choose the title for your thesis, report or paper, this is an ideal opportunity to allow yourself a bit of freedom. If you look at academic articles, there are several different ways a title can be structured. The most important thing is to make sure that the title actually reflects what you have written about, as the title is the very first thing that your supervisor and the person grading your thesis, report or paper will see, and this will give them the first impression about what to expect.

If you are writing a thesis, it is often possible to write a long title. Here is the title of my MSc thesis:

Qualitative and Quantitative Investigations into a Conceptual Model of Political Market Orientation

Yes, it's rather long, but the title does cover all of the contents of the thesis – I carried out both a qualitative investigation and a quantitative investigation of the concepts that made up a model of political market orientation. Think back to the Methodology and Method chapter in this book and my advice to focus on one method only in your paper – I didn't have the experience then that I do now.

An alternative is to use a title that is the complete opposite – that is, to create a title that consists of as few words as possible. At the extreme, you may have a textbook for one of your courses that consists of one word:

Marketing

Again, this does tell you all you need to know, especially when you see that the textbook is about 600 pages long . . .

In the middle are titles that are shorter but cover the area, sometimes as a sentence, and sometimes as a short question (for example, the research question). A specific type of title uses a colon to separate the title into two parts, where the first indicates the general area that your thesis, report or paper covers, and the second part indicates the specific focus:

Political Marketing: Theory and Concepts

This is the title of a book that I wrote with two colleagues. You can see that the first part of the title indicates the general area – Political Marketing – and the second part indicates the more specific topic – Theory and Concepts. Whatever title you choose, make sure that it is relevant to what you are writing about, and that the title is relatively short (so not like the title of my MSc thesis).

Abstract

An abstract is a very brief presentation of your thesis, report or paper that interested people can read in order to get an idea about what you have written. The abstract is often fewer than 250 words long, so you really have to think about which words you use to describe your thesis, report or paper, and how many words to use describing each part of your thesis, report or paper. One method of writing the abstract is to copy the Introduction and the Conclusion into a new document and see how many words you have. You will always have too many words, so it is time to start deleting words to get down to the right number. However, sometimes the number of words you are allowed is only 150. Here is an example of an abstract for this book in fewer than 150 words:

> This book gives advice to students in higher education on how to structure a thesis, report or paper. Using a generic structure of seven sections, this book demonstrates how to arrange a thesis, report or paper, leading to a more straightforward writing process so that supervisors and examiners can focus on the content of the student's work. Drawing on almost two decades of supervision experience, the author provides advice on how to avoid common mistakes that are made by those new to writing theses, reports and papers in higher education. Tips, tricks and best-practice examples are provided throughout the book. Finally, the book provides a template for structuring a paper.
>
> *110 words*

The type of thesis, report or paper that you are writing has an influence over which sections of the paper are emphasised. For example, if you are focusing on methodology and methods in a paper, then you can use more words on your methodology and method in the abstract. If we assume that this book was focused on the method of creating a structure for a semester paper, this is what the abstract would look like, in exactly 100 words:

This book focuses on how to structure a semester paper. The book uses a structure of seven sections to provide students with a straightforward way of integrating questions of methodology and method throughout their paper. The characteristics of a specific Methodology and Method section are presented, along with ideas for alternative paper structures that separate philosophy of science from the practical methods used in real-world investigations. An emphasis is placed on the impact of the chosen methodology and method on the structure of the entire paper, together with the importance of understanding the paper as one, integrated piece of writing.

100 words

Alternatively, if you are writing a thesis, report or paper for practitioners, then it is more important to focus on the implications of your research; if this book were focused on the implications of developing a structure for a written report in a commercial organisation, here is what the abstract would look like in fewer than 100 words:

This book focuses on how to structure a report for a commercial organisation. Using a generic structure of seven sections, this book provides practitioners with a straightforward way to develop a report that is laid out clearly, contains all of the information necessary, and can be used in multiple situations, from an executive summary to comprehensive strategy proposals based on rigorous research within target markets. Drawing on almost two decades of writing experience, the author provides a template for a report structure using practical examples, giving tips, tricks and advice on how to avoid common mistakes.

96 words

As you can see, all three of the short abstracts above can be applied to this book, with the only difference being the emphasis of the book. Of course, you are most likely a student in higher education who will use this book on a variety of courses, so the first abstract is the one that you will recognise. However, when you write a specific report or paper, you can use the second abstract to develop a structure that is appropriate to the course. Finally, when you are finished in higher education and get a job, you can look back through this book to get inspiration for the report that you are starting to write. Quite useful, right?

Keywords

Keywords are not normally part of writing a thesis, report or paper, but it is important to know what keywords are, their purpose and how to choose them. Keywords are precisely that – words that are key to understanding what you have written about. These keywords will be used by other people when searching for information about a particular topic, and it is possible for your thesis, report or paper – especially if it is a thesis – to be amongst the search results in a database of academic literature. However, sometimes you can be restricted to providing only three keywords, so you have to choose carefully. One keyword doesn't mean one word – it is possible to have more than one word per keyword. For example, here are three possible keywords for this book:

- Thesis structure
- Report writing
- Structuring a paper

As you can see, the keywords reflect a general description of the content of the book – don't try and be too specific, as you have to take into consideration who is trying to find your thesis, report or paper. They don't know exactly what your thesis, report or paper is about as they haven't found it, but you want to give them enough clues to find your work. The keywords are used together with the Title and the Abstract; in a database, the potential reader will look for keywords, their attention will be attracted by your title and the abstract will tell them whether what you have written is relevant to them.

Reporting back to a contributing organisation

Some theses, reports and papers are written after an internship in an organisation, or when an organisation has been kind enough to provide access to employees to carry out interviews, provide you with access to data or just been very helpful. If this is the case, then it is important to show that you appreciate their help because, after all, you probably wouldn't have such a good thesis, report or paper if it wasn't for them. There are two things that you should do here: acknowledge the assistance that the organisation has given you in your thesis, report or paper, and provide them with a copy of your thesis, report or paper with a short report or executive summary that outlines how you carried out your research, your conclusions and your recommendations for the organisation.

Acknowledging the help that the organisation has given you will take you about a minute to write and can be included as a footnote on the first page or as part of a dedicated acknowledgements section of your paper. Equally easy is sending the company a copy of your thesis, report or paper with a 'thank you' letter; both of these are just normal politeness but will create a good impression of you as a person.

Furthermore, you can write two documents that will be more useful to the organisation: a short report and an executive summary. The short report to the organisation follows the same, generic paper structure presented in this book; remember to adjust the weighting of each of the sections to suit the organisation, with a much greater emphasis on the practical implications of your conclusions. The executive summary is even shorter, maximum three pages, where you <u>very briefly</u> write the Introduction, then briefly present the theory, or model or concept; research process; and results or findings, and finally present the practical implications for the organisation in bullet-point format. This will probably be the most important part of your report for the organisation, and who knows, you may even be employed by the organisation after your studies to help implement your implications.

However, there are two issues that need to be considered when reporting back to an organisation. First of all, if you have interviewed some employees, you will most likely have anonymised their comments. This is usually not a problem with regard to the people grading your thesis, report or paper, as it is unlikely that they are employed by the organisation that you have collaborated with. However, it may be obvious to anyone who works for the organisation who has said what, and this may cause problems. So even though you have the best of intentions and promise anonymity to each person you interview, it may be better to simply offer a dedicated short report instead of your actual thesis, report or paper; the organisation can still benefit from reading a dedicated short report and an executive summary.

The second issue concerns confidentiality. If you have worked with more than one organisation whilst you have researched your thesis, report or paper, then reporting back to each of them will be more complicated, as you cannot simply give your whole thesis, report or paper to all of the organisations that helped you – this may give away industrial secrets and will most likely lead to problems for future students in getting data from the organisations, and in the worst case, legal action against you. If in doubt, ask your supervisor!

Checklists

Ask your supervisor
> . . . for some help in writing back to the company, if you were helped by one;
> . . . if you are in doubt about confidentiality issues.

Do's and don'ts
* DO remember that the structure presented in this book is a general structure – your thesis, report or paper may follow a different structure;
* DO report back to the organisation if you have been helped by one;
* DO consider your title if you are choosing your own – it does matter.

Common mistakes
* The title is too long or too short;
* The title and keywords do not reflect what is in the text;
* Not following your supervisor's advice.

Epilogue

This time, you *have* finished writing your thesis, report or paper – well done! Once you have enjoyed your well-earned break, you can reflect on the process of writing your thesis, report or paper. From an academic perspective, what have you learned from writing this paper? From a process perspective, what have you learned about writing your thesis, report or paper, and what would you do differently next time? These are important reflections, as you can use them when you start writing your *next* piece of work. In the context of this book, the appropriate question is, did the structure outlined in this book make writing your thesis, report or paper more straightforward?

You may be just starting out in higher education, and hopefully you will be able to use the structure in this book for other reports and papers, with any changes that reflect the subject of each course or that you or your supervisor think are necessary. It is this that I want to underline here at the end of this book – if you are uncertain, then always ask your supervisor. Show them this book, be prepared for them to say "I don't agree with what the book says", and then follow their advice. After all, they are the ones who are guiding you with your thesis, report or paper.

DOI: 10.4324/9781003334637-14

You can also think about this balance between what this book advises, what your supervisor advises and what you think yourself – it's an important skill to learn that you will continue to use once you leave higher education and get a job. If your manager asks you to write a report focusing on the implementation of a marketing strategy, you should not focus so much on the method, although you may want to include this in the report. The key questions are, who is going to read my report, why are they going to read my report, and what do they want to use my report for?

When all is said and done, I can guarantee you that developing a clear structure for your thesis, report or paper before you start writing will make the process more straightforward. It won't make your thesis, report or paper easier to write, as that depends on your abilities and the subject, but a structure will make the writing process more straightforward. You can use the tips and tricks, advice and template provided in this book to create this clear structure, but remember: listen to all advice, and then ignore two-thirds of it – but don't ignore what your supervisor says!

Good luck!

Index

Printed in the United States
by Baker & Taylor Publisher Services